Gwenllian,
The Welsh Warrior Princess

Peter Newton

ISBN: 0-86381-759-9

Cover design: Sian Parri
Cover illustrations: author/Bwrdd Croeso Cymru

First published in 2002 by
Gwasg Carreg Gwalch, 12 Iard yr Orsaf, Llanrwst, Wales LL26 0EH
℡ 01492 642031   ▤ 01492 641502
✆ books@carreg-gwalch.co.uk   Internet: www.carreg-gwalch.co.uk

This book is dedicated to my wife Lesley,
and my children Richard and Janine,
for their unconditional love and support.

ACKNOWLEDGEMENTS

The author would like to thank the following people for their kind assistance during the research and writing of this book:

Gabriella George, Eirian Harrison, Phyl Robson, Dai Owen, Elizabeth Smith (Gwenllian Farm), John Peace (Gwenllian Court Hotel), Ann Russell (Cydweli Castle), Myrddin and John and finally Joyce (my Mother).

CONTENTS

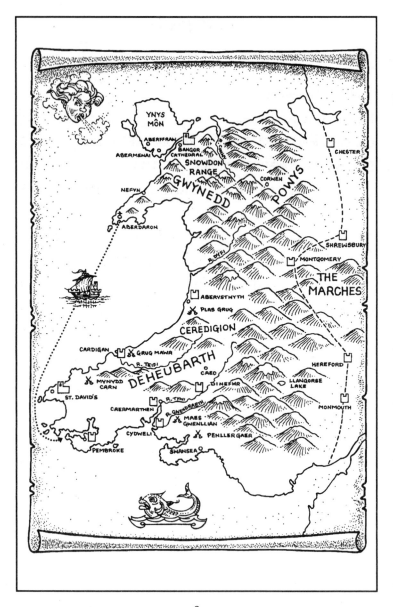

YNYS
MÔN

ABERFFRAW

ABERMENAI

BANGOR
CATHEDRAL

SNOWDON
RANGE

GWYNEDD

CORWEN

POWYS

CHESTER

NEFYN

ABERDARON

SHREWSBURY

R. DYFI

MONTGOMERY

ABERYSTWYTH

PLAS GRUG

THE
MARCHES

CEREDIGION

CARDIGAN

GRUG MAWR

R. TEIFI

DEHEUBARTH

HEREFORD

MYNYDD
CARN

CAEO

LLANGORSE
LAKE

ST. DAVID'S

DINEFWR

CAERMARTHEN

R. TYWI

MONMOUTH

GWENDRAETH

CYDWELI

MAES
GWENLLIAN

PENLLERGAER

PEMBROKE

SWANSEA

8

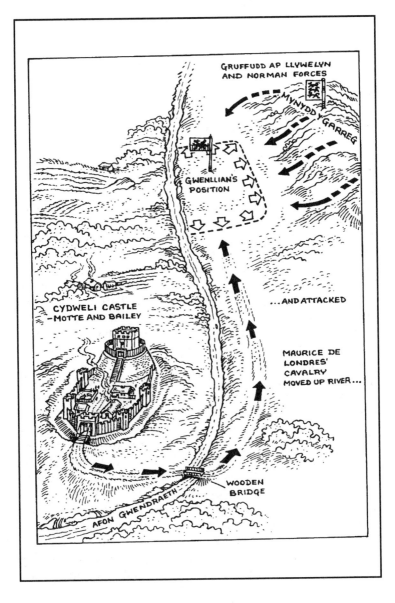

9

AUTHOR'S FOREWORD

Over the years, countless writers have toiled to bring stories that need telling to the notice of a wider public. The inspiration that is awoken on the first uncovering of some remarkable fact often becomes a true labour of love. If it were not so, then it is unlikely that the exploits of Scottish hero William Wallace or, in complete contrast, the brave and tragic story of Anne Frank told in her own words through her heart wrenching diaries, would have been brought to public attention. Living in these relatively peaceful times, one can only feel humbled by the extraordinary brave lives they led in the face of evil aggressors, hell-bent on their annihilation.

It is from this premise that I decided to record the life of a remarkable lady from our misty past. Her tale stirs up images of medieval life under the yoke of Norman aggressors, led by genocidal kings who were more than content to oversee the slaughter and subjugation of the last bastions of hope for the ancient Brythons, namely the Welsh people, or *Cymry*. The fact that I live in Gwynedd has certainly influenced me to re-tell her remarkable, yet tragic, story. It was then a kingdom and, although now only a county, Gwynedd still abounds with historical sites and battlefields on which our heroine's fair feet would have actually trodden.

Princess Gwenllian first came to my notice through *The Battles of Wales*, a book by Dilys Gater that gives only a brief account of her life, but it was enough to inspire me to dig a little deeper. The facts I uncovered through touring local, county and national libraries and consulting experts on medieval Wales, when combined with a little imagination, gave a detailed enough picture with which to write what is essentially a dramatic story. This is especially true when one links Gwenllian through love, and subsequently marriage, to Gruffudd ap Rhys, a Welsh prince described by Thomas Jefferey Llewelyn Prichard in his book *Heroines Of Welsh History* (1854) as being 'like the Welsh Wallace of Scotland in reputation and deeds'.

Yet, while this is above all other consideration a love story of almost fairy tale proportions, the grim reality of their lives soon destroys the glossy embellishment found in such tales. And although this work is intended to focus on the life of our heroic diva, it is impossible to relate it without affording equal attention to her husband's extraordinary parallel existence. From the day they met, their paths were inexorably entwined, creating a force that affected the very fabric of Welsh and Norman history. It is sobering enough to know that this story is about the true lives of our hero and heroine – that they actually lived, fought and died on and for their beloved Welsh soil in a desperate attempt to save it from careless invading forces. This is not a story that was conjured up in the mind of a romantic fictional script writer. Were it not for their dashing deeds, and the deeds of many others who also sacrificed their lives before and since our prince and princess exploded onto the historic landscape, it is likely that the Welsh people and their language would long ago have been ground into the dust, to be lost forever.

'But, didn't the Normans eventually conquer Wales?' one could ask. The answer is that, even after over two hundred years and much sacrifice, they only achieved partial success. For although the Normans peppered the landscape with their castles, the free spirit of the Welsh still endured. The Normans learnt that, although grossly outnumbered, the Welsh always fought with ferocity and unharnessed bravery. Eventually, they even attracted the admiration of their enemies. The same was true in 49AD when Roman invaders finally caught Caradog, a Brython leader whom they called Caractacus, after he waged a long and bloody campaign against them. With his family in-tow, he was taken to Rome to face the judgement of the emperor himself. Upon arrival, he probably anticipated a derisory ending by public execution or gladiatorial combat as his reward, both being standard methods of dispensing Roman justice. However, much to his surprise, he was greeted with respect and admiration. Tales of his exploits as a ferocious warrior and adversary had impressed the citizens of Rome to such an extent that their emperor decided to spare him and his family, allowing them to live in relative luxury in Rome itself.

This, in principle, also happened in Norman times, as is apparent from the tale of Gwenllian's father, Gruffudd ap Cynan of Gwynedd, being cordially invited to London by his old adversary, Henry 1 despite the Welsh king's pugilistic history of despatching Norman souls from their earthly bodies. It is partly because of the respect that they commanded, however tentative it may be, from refusing to lie down and accept annihilation that the Welsh, Scots and Irish have managed to hold on to their heritage and culture, and continue to do so even in the face of modern pressures that now come not only from England, but also from over the Atlantic ocean. The sacrifices of sons and daughters, fathers and mothers, have therefore not been entirely in vain, for the people live on as testament to their ancient histories.

There is, however, another reason I decided to undertake this project. I was dismayed to discover that when I approached my many Welsh-speaking friends with questions about Princess Gwenllian, most were oblivious to her existence. Indeed, I soon discovered, with the obvious exception of people at the premier centres of academic learning and those living in and around the town of Cydweli, between Caerfyrddin (Carmarthen) and

Llanelli, that this is probably true of most of the Welsh population. This saddens me, for it reflects the dark decades of history education in Wales when children and young people were taught little more than the lives and details of countless English, Russian, Prussian and French kings and queens as well as a prime minister and president or two, without mention of the proud history of their own country. Ask yourself, for example, how many children in the UK and much further afield, have not heard about the exploits of Robin Hood, a Saxon hero who may have existed, but probably didn't. Then ask yourself how many children outside of schools in Welsh-speaking areas or the dedicated Welsh language schools, have heard of a true, flesh and blood Welsh hero such as Owain Glyndŵr, a man whose greatest crime was to possess a vision for his beloved Wales that did not directly include England. You might well go on to ask whether any young people really want to know in this modern day and age. That question can easily be answered by studying the Scots reaction to the exploits of William Wallace becoming widely known through the medium of the movie *Braveheart*. Many of these 'hidden' historic events, shrouded in the distant past, are fascinating in their own right as action, adventure and romantic stories. There are of course many other such stirring traditional and cultural legends, if only we were made aware of them.

This work, however, is not intended as a monotone, historical textbook blandly spitting out facts and figures. On the contrary, I intend to bring to life the whole gamut of emotions experienced by those who lived in medieval Wales, and to that end it has unashamedly been dramatised.

Throughout time, the Welsh have re-lived and re-breathed the exploits of their legendary heroes. The Welsh people of the twelfth century had not yet tasted defeat and faced the oblivion of their race and tongue, for they knew that they were of privileged stock. These were not savages for they lived under a system of amicable and highly sophisticated laws that had evolved over many centuries and were codified one hundred and fifty years earlier by Hywel Dda, a wise and astute king. These laws helped to create a caring society that generally existed in peaceful cohabitation, undermined only by the traditional savagery that occurred in the wake of a Welsh sovereign's death. However, do not let this image of sublime cordiality fool you for, in the hearts of this proud nation beat a fervent and undying hope that, one day, they would recover their sacred Isle by driving out all foreign invaders at the end of a host of glinting spears.

The sources of information that carry accounts of Gwenllian and her family are, as was so often the case in medieval Wales when poets and the poetic system served as the memory of the nation, few and far between. However, just enough exists to track the course of her tumultuous life. Where clarity is wanting, I have applied my own imagination, based on fact, to illuminate what would otherwise be voids of uncertainty. For are we all not human and remain subjected to the same strengths and weaknesses of our ancestors? Can we not feel love, patriotism, despair and elation, just as they did? I leave it to the reader to decide as I unfold the life and times of the last Welsh warrior princess to grace this ancient land, Gwenllian.

INTRODUCTION

Life in Wales has never been easy. The country's distant past is bloody to say the least, littered as it is with relentless wars and sacrifice against aggressors who over many centuries have striven to drive the ancient Celts into extinction. This was the actual case in the Strathclyde region of Scotland where Anglo-Saxon expansionism destroyed the lives of the Welsh speaking inhabitants. It all came to a head at *Catraeth*, now known as Catterick, in the battle lamentably remembered in *Y Gododdin*, a long heroic poem written by the Welsh poet Aneirin in about the year 600. Although hopelessly outnumbered, over three hundred Welsh warriors stood their ground and gave their lives for a freedom that was becoming ever less of a certainty.

The Welsh knew from then on that if they did not stand firm, their enemies would forever perceive them as being weak. Their persecutors soon discovered that when they 'crossed the line', it cost them dearly. This line, however, was constantly moving west during the so called Dark Ages, and the Welsh were soon squeezed into a smaller and smaller patch of land until finally they all ended up on the mountainous western extremity that they called *Cymru*. Compare this to the western extremities of England, in Cornwall *(Cernyw)* and Cumbria, both of which were also at one time very much part of the greater Welsh/Cornish speaking collection of minor kingdoms. Offa went as far as building an early version of the Berlin Wall, this one between the estuaries of the Dee and the Wye, to keep the Welsh out of his kingdom in Mercia once and for all. By medieval times, Offa's Dyke roughly marked what friend and foe alike knew as the Welsh border, weaving its way like a dragon's tail from the gates of Chester in the north to link up with the sea at Monmouth in the south. West of this border was home to the mysterious *Cymry*, tough hardy people, who rejoiced then as indeed they do to this day, in their ancestral heritage and culture, having survived by living fully to the maxim, *Only through strength will you find peace*.

The Welsh however, largely due to their system of transferring property from generation to generation were plagued by internal squabbles that became a living thorn festering in their sides, much to the pleasure of their enemies. This lack of unity amongst the leaders and princes, so typical of the ancient Celtic races, was now to cost them dearly, for Wales was threatened by a new and sinister adversary, more cunning than any they had encountered before. Like a cancer, this new invader from the shores of Normandy brought with them their own dastardly brand of feudalism, that contrived to attack and annul the very core of Welsh society. They quickly learned where the greatest Welsh weakness lay and, aided by the old petty jealousies, sought to divide the Welsh by covert manipulation through deception, threats and bribery. Then like vultures, they stepped back to perch at a safe distance behind their border castle ramparts, gloating over their instigated bloody slaughter. Only when the dragon lay mortally wounded did they move to strip the bones of resistance, and therefore, gain their prize with minimal effort on their part, but at great cost to the Welsh.

Though they trespassed and administered their unjust governorship, they always suspected that they were only in Wales on borrowed time. An unpredictable storm could wrench their iron grip and cause them to lose everything that they gained should they foolishly ignore the warning signs. For if there was one lesson the enemies of the Welsh had painfully learned, it was that they dare not drop their guard whilst on

Welsh soil. The *Cymry*, a nation forged from centuries of conflict, would quickly strike back, and any martyrs killed during the struggle only inspired the dragon to bite even deeper the next time.

Thus a bitter contest ebbed and flowed like the tide. It began with the Norman King William 1, *the Conqueror*, following his 'epic' defeat of an already battle weakened Harold at Hastings in 1066. William set out on a course to brutally subjugate all the inhabitants of the British Isles and, having crushed the last remnants of Saxon resistance with tactics that could only be described as bordering on genocidal, he then turned his unmerciful attention to the western stronghold of the ancient Brythons – Cymru. He shirked direct confrontation however, resorting to installing unscrupulous Marcher barons in the strategic sites of Chester, Shrewsbury, Hereford and Monmouth. Not at any time did William 'plan' to conquer Wales. He simply told the barons where their eastern borders lay, and left it to them to decide where exactly they wanted to place their western borders. The barons then waited for opportune moments to strike against north, south or central Wales, as circumstances dictated. William had enough to occupy his mind, what with political intrigues in London and threats from his native Normandy, so he was content to leave the troublesome Welsh to his agents. English historians have always made much of the divisive nature of the Welsh. What all have failed to point out is that the Welsh of the north, the central parts, and the south hardly ever had a common enemy after this time. They always had to be on their guard, for the barons were as greedy and as bloody a set of local government officials as ever walked this ancient land. By their irreverent actions, these barons became the key players in the fateful tapestry of events leading to the tragedy that befell Gwenllian, her family and the nation.

It is no coincidence that the terms *Norman* and *Norsemen* appear to be similar. Norman ancestors were in fact Vikings, who had settled in that area of northern France that is called

Normandy as lately as 911AD, and endemic as it was to Scandinavians of that time, they instinctively sought and practiced 'aggressive expansionism'. They were undoubtedly a very warlike people, who positively revelled in the challenge of invasion and drank heartily on the subsequent power that conquest could bring.

In order to achieve total domination, William granted his border overlords virtually limitless powers to propagate his war on the Welsh. This unmoderated governorship far outweighed the limited powers he had granted their counterparts who resided in conquered Saxon England. Behaving like subsidiary kings of their own territories, the Marcher Lords freely murdered, pillaged and raped the Welsh, confiscating all the land and chattels they could, more or less as it pleased them unless they faced stern opposition from the 'troublesome' Welsh. On the rare occasions when total occupancy of an area was complete, they ethnically cleansed the zone and replaced the natives with their own domesticated vassals who were mainly of Flemish or Saxon descent. There were some exceptions however, for native Welshmen who were of use were forced into subservience to feed the great Norman war machine. The two nations that now faced each other were divided by language, principles, ethics and culture. One was regarded as having the most powerful and modern army in Europe whilst the other boasted natural born fighters, trained in the warrior arts from early childhood, much like the Spartans of ancient times.

Amidst this mayhem, as early as 1081 two powerful figures rose from the ashes of a great civil struggle that took place on Welsh soil at Mynydd Carn, near Trefdraeth (Newport) in Penfro (Pembrokeshire). Gruffudd ap Cynan and Rhys ap Tewdwr, the victors of this epic two-day long bloodbath, were to become the fathers of the lead players in this drama. Both firmly believed themselves to be the rightful heirs to the kingdoms of Gwynedd in the north and Deheubarth in the south respectively. Gruffudd, however, would always eclipse his southern counterpart. One reason for this was Gruffudd ap Cynan's claim that he was the mighty king of Welsh and Viking blood, as foretold by the wizard *Myrddin* (Merlin), centuries earlier.

Gruffudd and Rhys had agreed to join forces to overthrow the would-be usurpers mustering against them, led by Trahaearn ap Caradog, then lord of Arwystli, Ardudwy and Meirionnydd, Caradog ap Gruffudd of Gwent and Meilir ap Rhiwallon of Powys. These men were all considered traitors by their own race, especially when they were seen in possession of Norman-supplied arbalesters. These machines of war would inflict terrible injuries on any poor souls unfortunate enough to be in the line of fire. When Gruffudd and Rhys saw such deadly weapons, they must have felt less certain as to whether they would ever gain their rightful crowns.

Facing this powerful throng of rival Welshmen, Rhys gathered a band of loyal men from Deheubarth. Although Gruffudd's force vastly outnumbered Rhys's, they were in the main made up of seasoned Irish and Danish mercenaries supplemented by loyal men of Gwynedd. The ensuing battle raged for two whole days, during which all three rival opponents were slain along with most of their followers. This joint and mutually rewarding victory firmly cemented a close friendship between the two kings, who had now become the most powerful rulers in Wales. Gruffudd returned to Gwynedd to embark on a rebuilding programme to fire the loyalty and spiritual fibre of his people. By strengthening the previously weakened infrastructure, he hoped to create a strong defendable fortress behind which his nation could prosper. In southern Wales, Rhys had also set about the re-establishment of Deheubarth, no doubt anxious to consolidate his gains. However, within six months of his northern ally's triumphant return to Gwynedd, news reached Rhys of Gruffudd's arrest and imprisonment by the bellicose Norman Earl of Chester,

Hugh of Avranches, alias Hugh the Fat. Gruffudd had been presented on a platter to his enemies through the betrayal and trickery of a local Welsh leader known as Meirion Goch *(the Red)* who, ironically, had been the first leader to welcome the young sovereign when he had landed at Abermenai some years earlier. One can only surmise that he must have felt the ambitious prince's arrival posed a threat to his own local power-base. So, with pockets undoubtedly lined with Norman gold, he duped Gruffudd into attending what he portrayed as a peace conference in Corwen. Believing it to be the best course of action for his beleaguered and divided subjects, the inexperienced but well meaning king reluctantly accepted the invitation. Upon his arrival, the trap was sprung. A huge force of Norman knights completely overwhelmed his small guard. He was immediately despatched to Chester, while his escort of loyal Irish *teulu* (personal bodyguards) were released only after the Normans had relieved them of their thumbs. This was a common practice that ensured the victim could never again raise a sword or draw a bow against them. One can almost feel the smug sense of achievement in Hugh's party as they made their way back to Chester, having netted the only major threat to Norman control over the whole of northern Wales.

After safely depositing the Welsh king in a high security cell deep in the bowels of Chester Castle, Hugh and his first lieutenant Robert of Rhuddlan, led a large force into Gwynedd to destroy the north Wales stronghold, driving the king's wife, Angharad along with her retinue into exile in Ireland. Historians seem to be divided at this point, some claiming that Gruffudd was held in prison for eight years and others saying twelve. However, the date of his dramatic escape does present a clearer picture; everyone unanimously agreeing that it occurred in the year 1094. One can safely assume that, throughout his long penal servitude, many attempts were made to free him from his Norman jailers, which possibly explains why they adopted a policy of moving him from jail to jail at a moment's notice. The practical ramification of what in theory seemed like a good idea, proved to be fortuitous for his supporters in the long run.

Gruffudd eventually won his freedom, not by pardon or amnesty, but from the daring actions of a young Welsh trader named Cynwrig Hir, who heralded from Edeirnion in Powys. He undoubtedly saved the king from almost certain death in the filthy Norman cells. Cynwrig was conducting his usual business in a busy Chester street market, when he recognised the frail, sorry-looking, manacled and fettered man who was being escorted down the street as Gruffudd ap Cynan. Although it is likely Cynwrig's loyalty lay with the Powys royals, no doubt he would still have been vexed at the sight of a fellow countryman being treated so shabbily, especially by the Normans. Forced to contain his anger for fear of his own life, he followed the group on horseback at a discreet distance until they stopped at a roadside inn.

Having tethered the king to a horse ring with a leather strap, and making him to sit on the floor amidst the horse dung and dust, the soldiers disappeared inside to share a flagon of ale for their parched throats.

With heart pounding and adrenalin rushing through his veins, Cynwrig grasped his chance with both hands, and cut the king's ties. Swinging him up onto his broad shoulders, Cynwrig ran the short distance to where he had hidden his horse. Carefully placing the weak king on the horse's back, he sped off at a gallop, even then not fully appreciating the enormity of what he had done in those few seconds. He was, however, elated in the knowledge that he had achieved what many of his fellow countrymen had failed to do; free a king of the Welsh. As the soldiers were only on foot, they had no chance of catching the pair who, when the alarm was raised, became the most wanted men in Wales. Initially Cynwrig hid the king in his own home, but then with the aid of friends spread throughout the *cantrefi* (hundreds) between Chester and Afon Conwy, and by travelling at night, they made good their escape. Despite a massive search, a furious Hugh was unable to trace his prize prisoner. The complacent guards who allowed the Welsh king to escape evidently paid for their mistake with their lives. Within a couple of months, however, Gruffudd was reunited with his family in Dublin.

Tragically just a year earlier, Gruffudd ap Cynan's staunch southern ally, Rhys ap Tewdwr, was captured and beheaded by the Norman protagonist Bernard Neufmarche at Talgarth near Afon Wysg (the River Usk) in Brycheiniog (Brecknockshire). The elderly, yet obviously still game, Rhys died as a true warrior would have wished, whilst defending the western boundary of his beloved Deheubarth. To this day the specific location where the soul of the brave prince of Deheubarth left its earthly form is remembered as 'Pen Rhys' *(Rhys's Head)*. This lamentable event heralded the break-up of his principality, especially after his two eldest sons, Gorono and Cynan, had met the same fate as their father whilst leading the remnants of the once mighty Deheubarth forces. Thankfully his two remaining infant sons, Gruffudd and Hywel along with their elder sister Nest, survived the bloodletting. However, despite his youngest sons' ages, the fact that they were rightful claimants to the crown of Deheubarth left them in mortal danger, especially from rival Welsh leaders.

At this time history records that young Gruffudd ap Rhys was removed to Ireland and placed under protection of King Murcart of Dublin, where he remained until the age of twenty-five. During his enforced exile, Gruffudd received training in the warrior arts and court etiquette, both essential learning for a would-be prince of a volatile south Wales. His mother Gwladus, daughter of Rhiwallon ap Cynfryn fails to receive a mention at this dramatic crossroads in her children's lives; did she also flee to Ireland with Gruffudd, or did she remain in Wales with Nest and Hywel? That, alas, is yet another unresolvable mystery from Wales's turbulent past. It appears that Hywel and Nest did remain in Wales, the former eventually being captured and imprisoned by the Normans, and the latter becoming the wife of the powerful Norman lord Gerald de Windsor. However this was not before her beauty had caught the eye of King Henry I who took her for his mistress and to whom, it is believed, she bore an illegitimate child.

Meanwhile, by the end of 1094, Gruffudd ap Cynan had returned to Welsh shores, leading a sizeable force of Irish and Danish mercenaries, once again intent on reclaiming his occupied kingdom. He and his men set down from a fleet of Danish ships at Nefyn on the Llŷn Peninsula, where they stormed the local Norman castle and put all of its one hundred and twenty-four defenders to the sword. News of this inspired the men of Gwynedd, who rushed to his side and again swore allegiance to the king before embarking on a campaign that razed to the ground every Norman-held castle west of Afon Conwy.

By the end of the revolt, the bruised, bloody and exhausted men of Gwynedd, with substantial help from the mercenaries, had once again restored much of Wales to a Welsh king. Meirion Goch's fate is unknown, although one might not be too far off in assuming that the one who had betrayed his king thirteen years previously could soon expect to feed the fish of the Menai Straits. Unfortunately, any ideas Gruffudd had of expanding his borders were halted by the heir to the Norman throne of England, William Rufus. He clearly showed that he lacked none of the shrewdness and mettle of his father. When news of what he saw as an insurrection resulting in the slaughter of Norman knights reached the man recorded by the Anglo-Saxon Chronicles as, 'to nearly all his people hateful and abominable to God', he flew into a rage. Immediately he set about raising a host of avenging Norman angels, all motivated to annihilate the rampaging Welshmen, who even had the audacity to enter England and lay waste to large areas of Cheshire and Shropshire.

By late October 1095 William was on Welsh soil driving all before him, including Gruffudd ap Cynan who retreated to his mountain stronghold west of Afon Conwy. The timing of William's expedition was ill-fated, as would many others in the ensuing centuries. The reliable winter dragon of the *Cymry* of the north blew her icy breath on his forces, blasting them back through the gates of Chester.

In the south however, William continued to drive home the attack against Cadwgan ap Bleddyn and his men of Ceredigion and Dyfed who, in conjunction with Gruffudd ap Cynan's northern thrusts, had driven out most of the Norman occupiers of mid and South Wales. Nevertheless, such were the forces now waged against Cadwgan, that he decided to negotiate terms resulting in his swearing fealty to William, thereby stabbing his northern ally in the back.

However, gradually between 1095 and 1097, Gruffudd managed to consolidate what he had recovered and returned to Aberffraw on Ynys Môn, to the historic and principal site of the royal court of the sovereigns of Gwynedd. After years of neglect the place was badly in need of repair and restoration, as indeed was the whole of the *Maerdref* (royal estate). The king strove to achieve self-sufficiency, though initially supplemented by goods imported on merchant ships mostly from Ireland, that would moor at the mouth of Afon Ffraw. He believed that if left unmolested to prosper in Welsh hands, Aberffraw could become a self contained, harmonious and wealthy society.

Within weeks, Gruffudd had commissioned a *Degion* (King's council) to assist him in running the affairs of his kingdom. The *Degion* was formed from trusted leaders and nobles of Gwynedd, who were collectively known as y *Gwŷr Da* (good men). With their help, the transformation of the palace and estates became a reality over the ensuing months and life returned to a semblance of relative normality.

However, normality in any land bordering with England meant 'expect the unexpected' and in 1097 William II, frustrated by his previous aborted foray, decided to regain his much weakened credibility by revisiting Welsh soil with his armed forces. Unfortunately, he had obviously not learnt anything from his previous campaign and once again returned across the border badly bruised and beaten. From this time he decided to leave Wales to his barons, who were commissioned to embark on an unprecedented programme of constructing heavily fortified castles, from which they could eliminate all resistance and thereby control the 'unruly' Welsh.

CHAPTER ONE

"BORN INTO TURMOIL"
1097 - 1114

In the year 1097, in the face of the grave threat to the lives of her family, Gruffudd ap Cynan's wife Angharad (the Fair) gave birth to the last of her eight children. To her was born a beautiful baby girl whom she named *Gwenllian*; a child that would grow into a powerful leader and whose influence would provide a spark to set Wales alight. She had four older sisters called Mared, Rhiannell, Susanna and Annest about whom little is recorded, for they were soon to be eclipsed by their baby sister. In addition, she had three brothers in Cadwallon, Owain and Cadwaladr, from whom she would learn so much to prepare her for the challenges ahead.

Life in Aberffraw at the time of her birth was tense, especially when her father learned that William II planned to invade for a second time. The palatial life that Gwenllian's family was only settling into was soon substituted for a more peasant-like existence high in *Eryri* (the Snowdonia mountains). From there Gruffudd ap Cynan conducted a guerilla war that would eventually prove fruitful in the outcome.

When William had been embarrassed for a second time by his lack of knowledge of both his adversaries and of the conditions, Gruffudd, Angharad and the young family returned to Aberffraw to pick up the pieces from where they had left off

in the rebuilding programme. Gwenllian was too
appreciate the stresses her parents lived under. Ho
dour atmosphere of court life would soon have dissipa
sound of children's laughter, which would never have
away in the modestly constructed buildings. Built of ...wer
frame supplied from the well-stocked oak forests of Ynys Môn,
these buildings had wattle and daub walls and sloping thatched
bracken roofs overlaid with turf that acted as a waterproof
membrane that withheld the harshest of weather.

In addition to his children born to Angharad, the
promiscuous Gruffudd also sired others to courtesans. While
this was an enjoyable pastime for most kings, there was no
doubt that such illicit behaviour often become the source of
future domestic conflict, and not only from irate queens, for
legitimate and illegitimate sons coveted the crown alike.

Even at this early stage of her life, Gwenllian is singled out
in a poem reputed to have been written by the court bard
Meilyr. He records in simple verse the affection reserved for her
at the time:

Sleep, Gwenllian, my heart's delight
Sleep on through shivering spear and brand,
An apple rosy red within thy baby hand;
Thy pillowed cheeks a pair of roses bright,
Thy heart as happy day and night!
Mid all our woe, O! vision rare!
Sweet little princess cradled there,
Thy apple in thy hand thy all of earthly care.

Thy brethren battle with the foe,
Thy Sire's red strokes around him sweep,
Whilst thou, his bonny babe, art smiling through thy sleep.
All Gwalia shudders at the Norman blow!
What are the angels whispering low
Of thy father now?

Bright babe, asleep upon my knee,
How many a queen of high degree
Would cast away her crown to slumber thus like thee!

The deep sense of love surrounding the baby girl positively oozes from this delightful poem. Plainly she was a pleasant distraction from the horrors of war that beat upon her father's door. It was as if they already sensed that she would be exalted, not only from amongst her siblings, but her people too.

In 1098, two powerful Marcher Earls both called Hugh, one of Chester and one of Shrewsbury, joined forces in a determined effort to subdue Aberffraw, Ynys Môn and subsequently the whole of north Wales. They attacked by land and sea with forces far superior to anything that Gruffudd ap Cynan could raise. During this time was seen a particularly poignant demonstration of the lack of loyalty amongst royal family members; Owain and Uchtryd, brothers of Angharad and lords of *Tegeingl* (a region containing the verdant lands between the River Dee and Afon Clwyd) assisted her enemies by providing them with strategically sensitive information on Gruffudd ap Cynan's troop numbers and defence capabilities. They also offered safe passage through their own territories to the Norman land forces. The dishonour that was brought upon Angharad's family was eventually avenged when, in 1124, her youngest son Cadwallon slew both his uncles.

With little choice left open to him, Gruffudd and his family fled to Ireland and sought the aid of King Magnus, the powerful Norwegian monarch who had already subjugated the Orkneys, the Isle of Man and most of the islands off the west coast of Scotland. It appears he was moved when told of the barbaric behaviour the Normans had inflicted upon the natives of Ynys Môn. He therefore set sail with a large Viking force to oust all Normans from the island. This task was made so much easier when, upon arrival, he despatched Hugh of Shrewsbury to an early grave with a single arrow shot from his own hands. The premature death of Hugh's totally demoralised his forces and they left the island in great haste, fearful of the likely back-lash after their unsolicited savagery on the natives, leaving the door open for a speedy return of an equally depressed Gruffudd ap Cynan. Magnus received his just rewards for returning Gwynedd into Welsh hands and left the now weakened king to his own devices. By the end of the century, the Normans in north Wales had retreated behind a line drawn by Afon Conwy, whilst they held in south Wales Penfro (Pembrokeshire), Morgannwg (Glamorganshire), Gwynllŵg and Brycheiniog (Brecknockshire). Again Gwenllian's frustrated father established his seat of power in smouldering Aberffraw, and with grit and determination he rebuilt it, only this time stronger than ever, swearing never to be driven from the island again.

Gradually over the years, Gwenllian grew to cast a blaze of colour across a grey canvas of war, bloodshed and fear. The qualities and personality of this beacon of hope would have been like a breath of fresh air amidst the polluted climate of Norman aggression. While she was a loving and caring person, she had also been gifted with the fiery temperament that her father was renowned for. Yes, one could accurately describe her as the *tom boy* of the royal princesses, causing distress to some with her contemptible pranks, yet attracting love and admiration from others being a pretty blue eyed scamp of a girl with her long blonde ringlets bobbing up and down as she ran circles around the courtiers.

From about the age of six, this bundle of energy began to observe her brother's daily routine of sports and arms practice, watching them compete in feats of strength including running, riding, jumping, swimming and wrestling, all under the tutelage of their father's men. For a royal princess there were the more mundane and gentler pastimes, such as embroidery, weaving, sowing and tuition in court etiquette, music and languages. However, Gwenllian would have been fit to burst if she had been restricted from joining her brothers in their vastly more enjoyable pastimes.

With a flash of her big blue eyes, shimmering with the beauty of a cobalt sea, she had no trouble in persuading her father to let her join them. Thus began her training in the arts of the Welsh warriors. With time and a patient tutor, she became proficient with the sword, bow and lance and could ride a horse as well as any of her male counterparts. After all, in times of war, etiquette goes out the window. Here was a warrior child born of a warrior family and, as far as her wise and liberal minded father was concerned, an unforgiving assassin's blade does not distinguish between male and female flesh. Life in the royal household was still a little restrictive at times for the young princess, but it was not long before she was learning noble falconry and joining her brothers on hunts, pursuing larger game like deer or wild boar. In the evenings she joined her brothers and sisters in the king's hall for their supper and enjoyed having her bare feet licked by the friendly Irish wolfhounds, which lay patiently beneath the banquet table waiting for the scraps of food tossed down by their masters. Afterwards she would lie down on warm bear-skin rugs placed before a roaring peat or log fire, particularly inviting during the winter months. From this enviable position, she would listen with wide-eyed innocence to various members of the household recounting dashing tales of Welsh heroism, adventure and intrigue, all culminating with a vibrant feast of music and verse from Meilyr Brydydd, the court poet.

Later when safely tucked up in a large freshly compacted straw bed overlaid with a soft woollen blanket, that she shared with her sister, she would snuggle down under the warm quilted coverlet and drift off into a deep refreshing night's sleep, disturbed only by the occasional haunting sound of a wolf's cry, still audible through the heavy timber shutters that sealed the window opening.

William II had died anomalously in August 1100 whilst hunting in the New Forest. His demise was officially described as an accident. The superficial period of mourning for this unpopular king, whose tyrannical father had met a similar end, brought to a close a short and misguided reign – tyrants and despots seem incapable of learning from past mistakes that were perpetrated by their kind. Those who wield a bloody sword almost invariably find it turned against them. William's death came as a blessing to the Welsh resistance leaders who now seemingly had valuable time to regroup and bolster their defences, but their respite was abruptly interrupted by the speedy succession to the throne of William's younger and more energetic thirty-two year old brother Henry, a mere three days after the so-called accident. The fact that Henry was a member of the hunting party on that fateful day begs the question as to whom rather than what they were hunting?

Henry I wasted no time in continuing his predecessor's encroachment into Wales by placing Flemish settlers in Rhos, Ceredigion, Talacharn and Cydweli. Between 1107 and 1110 what had started as a trickle gradually became a flood for, although his initial policy was to offer the Flemish colonialists barren or waste land, soon the incursion bled over into the more lucrative Welsh held lands. Here Henry adopted an indiscriminate ethnic cleansing stance through using force to drive noble freemen and bondmen, along with their respective slaves, from their lands.

The signs were not promising for Gwenllian and her people, who had hoped to enjoy a less oppressive lifestyle under this new Norman monarch of England. Welsh hopes sunk even further upon hearing news of Henry's steely spirit in the face of a rebellion led by his powerful brother Robert, Duke of Normandy. Robert invaded England in 1101, with the intention of wresting the crown from Henry's grasp. The shrewd king initially negotiated a stand-off, whereby Robert agreed to stall his challenge in return for Henry's substantial assets in Normandy. However, by September 1106, Henry's English based forces had grown sufficiently to mount a full scale invasion of Normandy, with the intention of destroying his brother's power base.

These events would have been of vital concern to Gruffudd ap Cynan and allies such as Cadwgan ap Bleddyn, Lord of Powys and Ceredigion. As if to dampen the resurgence of their aspirations, news that Henry was returning as King of England and Duke of Normandy following his decisive victory in the Battle of Tinchebrai, fought near Avranches, came as a bitter blow. There he had captured and blinded Robert, who was to die incarcerated in a filthy Norman cell some twenty-eight years later.

CHAPTER TWO

"A FREE-SPIRIT"
1113 – 1114

By 1113, Gwenllian was in the fruit of her youth and catching the eye of many potential suitors in Gwynedd and no doubt in other friendly and not so friendly provinces. She was blessed with unsurpassed beauty and spirit that in itself drew the attention of noble enquirers. Besides these obvious attractions, he who won her hand also gained access to the most powerful dynasty in the whole of Wales. This in itself was a good and just reason for her parents to protect her innocence, and also to take great care when considering and screening any candidates for potential benefits to the kingdom before sanctioning her courting. Traditionally, princesses had to obediently follow the path of pre-arranged marriages, whereby young impressionable girls were forced into wedlock with lords, nobles or princes of rival or supporting provinces. If love blossomed within such a treaty, it was considered a bonus. This was especially so for the woman, who was expected to stay faithful to her man although he could, and often did, cavort with any woman he liked. Then, as is the case today within cultures where arranged marriages are still practiced, the pleas of the spirited bride would fall on deaf ears as they were forced into a life of potential misery. Gwenllian was one such spirit who had, contrary to her father's views, decided to marry for the sake of love alone, as could the daughters of freemen and serfs. Gruffudd ap Cynan, however, was a strict authoritarian when it came to matters that could affect the prosperity of his kingdom. Thus were the seeds of discontent sown as two like-minded, stubborn players in a real life game of chess were set to clash over a knight and his manoeuvres on the chequered board of political intrigue and power.

This was the year in which Gruffudd ap Rhys, son of Gruffudd ap Cynan's southern ally, returned to Wales as the rightful heir to Deheubarth following twenty-five years in exile in Ireland. He was only a boy when he left, and he returned a man. He had been thoroughly exposed to an Irish lifestyle that had tempered him into the type of tough leader that Wales needed at that time. He had not been taught airs and graces, but he knew how to fight for and to take what was rightfully his. The tall, handsome and dashing warrior-prince with his thick black shoulder length wavy hair and short neatly cropped beard, presented himself with a handful of followers at the door of Pembroke Castle, home of his beautiful sister Nest who was by then the wife of the Norman lord, Gerald de Windsor. Such was the love that Gerald had for his raven haired sensual wife that he turned a blind eye to the fact that a mortal enemy now resided under his roof. Nest provided her brother with all the latest court news on her lover, Henry I, while an ever increasingly nervous Gerald looked on. For if news ever reached Henry that Gerald was harbouring the son of Rhys ap Tewdwr, it was likely that his head would roll. Gruffudd rejoiced in the news that his younger brother Hywel was still alive, and steadfastly resolved to free him from his custodial existence at Montgomery Castle. Faced by her husband's displeasure, Nest provided her brother with money, horses and general provisions before Gruffudd and his colleagues journeyed to an isolated and inhospitable district known as Caeo, nestling in the highest reaches of Cantref Mawr's craggy moorland and dense forests. Gruffudd was sustained in his roving outlaw existence by the generosity of his sister and his uncle Rhydderch ap Tewdwr who owned a respectable holding in Cantref Mawr. He, like his niece Nest, had to conduct all dealings with Gruffudd through the 'back door' for fear of reprisal.

It was from here that Gruffudd sent word for the loyal forces of Deheubarth to gather under his banner, in order to assist him in regaining his father's lost kingdom. Unfortunately, he had been ill-advised on his people's appetite for war, most of which had been beaten out of them by their Norman overlords. His frustration and anger was palpable when he gazed at the few supporters who journeyed to his mountain hideout. Though noble and patriotic in their intentions, they were a pitiful contrast to his father's once feared and numerous warriors. Twenty-five years was a long time since his father's dynasty had ruled the region and now he had before him a new generation that lacked the confidence of their fathers.

Through the well established network of spies that he had established in Deheubarth, Henry I soon knew of Gruffudd ap Rhys's intentions. Therefore, Henry despatched instructions to his regional representatives (Gerald de Windsor amongst them) to capture this potentially irritating rebel, dead or alive. In this way, a deadly cat and mouse game began that left the young prince militarily impotent and having to live with the constant threat of assassination.

By 1114 Henry, who was now regarded as the most powerful monarch in Europe, flexed his military might by announcing his intention to invade north and mid-Wales to exterminate the last threads of Welsh resistance. Whether he was sincere about this threat or just fearmongering is hard to tell, but it certainly had the desired effect on the two targets of his aggression. Gruffudd ap Cynan and the troublesome Owain ap Cadwgan of Powys and Ceredigion took Henry's feudal preparations seriously enough to effectively join and strategically gather their forces in the relative safety of Snowdonia, from where they could mount a typical Welsh guerilla war on their persecutors.

The trials and tribulations suffered by the Cymry during this, and previous campaigns of the Norman kings, were tremendous. The Normans showed nothing but contempt for the pawns who were forced to flee their homes in fear of their lives. Those who escaped were extremely lucky for, if captured, they would be subjected to barbaric torture and murder. As has been seen many times throughout history, a killing frenzy would spread like a plague through the advancing troops, this being an inexplicable phenomenon conceived in the battle zone that brings to the surface the most disgusting and depraved side of human nature. Even in their contemplative years long after such horrible events, the perpetrators of these actions lamented in silent and tortuous disbelief as to how they could sink to such a level, to which wild animals would never stoop.

As she sat astride her favourite horse accompanied by her family at the head of a column of refugees numbering in their thousands, all fleeing to the Welsh mountains, the teenage Gwenllian was deeply worried that these rampaging lions were on their way to savage her people. As it turned out, her trepidation of the unfolding events proved to be correct, for facing them was a formidable force of not one, but three armies led by Henry himself, Scottish King Malcolm and The Earl of Cornwall who now collectively converged on Gruffudd ap Cynan and Owain ap Cadwgan. Finally cornered by this overwhelming host, the Welsh leaders were forced to capitulate despite the pleas of Gwenllian to continue the fight. Her's was a voice amongst many young patriotic warriors who were prepared to lay down their lives to conserve their freedom. However, the wise and experienced head of her father prevailed and Henry retired after a hastily arranged face to face meeting with his adversaries who, without exception, surrendered and paid him homage. The shrewd Norman king had no intention of exterminating his captives, because he knew that his needs were best served by abstracting heavy tributes from them to help pay for the huge war machine he was obliged to maintain. He correctly surmised that Gwynedd would prosper untainted while Gruffudd remained in power, compared to the expectations of poor and erratic growth under a Norman localised governor, faced with a workforce low in moral and likely to revolt. Henry therefore sensed that he would be better leaving Gruffudd to his own devices. However, young Owain was not blessed with the same rational mind as his ageing ally who had suffered many years of hardship and sacrifice. His cavalier and irrational behaviour was the talk of Wales at the time, and of the many daring deeds he had undertaken, none were to match his renowned abduction of Nest, his second cousin and sister of young Gruffudd ap Rhys. In 1109 he had enlisted the help of a band of fellow romantic and reckless young warriors to join him on a raid on Pembroke Castle. It was a large motte and bailey timber structure of high wooden palisades, interrupted intermittently by circular watch towers, behind which was situated the inner keep, where Nest and her husband resided. He had been driven to partake in this reckless scheme out of frustration and a lust for adventure upon hearing of Nest's astounding beauty, that to him seemed wasted on her Norman husband. Gaining access through a tunnel dug under the outer defences, they quickly overpowered the guard and ran off with their prize. Gerald was away at the time, but when he returned to find his wife and personal chattels stolen, he raised a large cavalry based force that, during the search for Nest, wreaked havoc on innocent Ceredigion natives who were reputed to be assisting and hiding Owain. Such was Gerald's wrath that Owain was eventually forced to flee to Ireland and Nest returned to Pembroke, none the worse for her experience. However, this daredevil prince was soon back terrorising Norman and Flemish settlers alike which is why, to prevent any further trouble, Henry invited Owain (forcibly according to some accounts) to join him on a military expedition to France where he could keep an eye on him. Just like his fellow countrymen who had fought alongside Normans before,

Owen's prowess with sword, spear and bow was fully matched by his bravery in the heat of battle. A highly impressed Henry therefore duly knighted him in the hope of keeping such a valuable asset on his side.

With Owen safely tucked away in France the only remaining fly in the ointment was the Deheubarth prince who was by then responsible for numerous minor skirmishes. Henry stoked up the heat by placing the bounty on his head, and this ultimately became too much of a burden for Gruffudd to carry. So, with a heavy heart he disbanded his small group of followers and fled north to seek the protection of his father's old ally.

CHAPTER THREE

"LOVE AND BETRAYAL"
1114 - 1116

By the end of the year, life had again returned to normal for the by now weakened kingdom of Gwynedd. Repairs to the court and surrounding buildings were not necessary as Henry, in his haste to surround the Welsh forces in their mountain fastness in Snowdonia, had not ventured as far as Aberffraw on this occasion. The land tillers had returned to their homes and begun working the soil in order to prepare it for next year's crops of corn and oats. To help them through the coming winter, provisions were shipped in from Ireland and even Chester, now that there was a thawing in the bitter relationship with the Normans.

The substantial acreage of rich deciduous forest on Ynys Môn that had not been cleared for agricultural purposes, were more than able to provide local game for the pot. Thankfully, the desperation that had so recently filled their hearts now dwindled to a flicker and was replaced with a sense of relief that they had survived a potential holocaust. In the damp early morning air, dancing wisps of hot steam escaped the apex of the corn kiln and rose high above the skyline. House slaves hung out washing on lines that were strung up between the kitchens and the timber palisades. Babies cried while dogs barked and soldiers argued over duty rotas. Thing were indeed returning to normal.

ı morally enlightened Gwenllian, without
n with daily chores that were normally the
nts, ignoring stern looks and discerning
fellow royals. No longer did she walk the path
r the recent episode with Henry's forces had
mind to realise that all people are the same.
ı or slave, all bodies bleed and die. In the evenings
the sou.. music, story telling and poetic verse filled the once
sombre voids of the king's hall again. As the mood of the
settlement lightened, so did the attitude to clothing, as softer
and more colourful garments were adorned, instead of the
heavy martial leathers which were consistently worn in times of
peril.

Along the main arterial road from the direction of Aber
Menai, three riders approached the royal hamlet. Immediately
the king's men rode out to intercept them and, having
established whether they were friend or foe, escorted them into
the royal enclosure. They were none-other than young Gruffudd
ap Rhys and two of his loyal Deheubarth men, who had
accompanied him on the arduous and dangerous trek to the
friendly kingdom. The king was informed of the arrival of his
allies and cordially invited them into his hospitality.

This charismatic prince who had already developed a
reputation to rival that of Owain ap Cadwgan, sought two
things from Gruffudd ap Cynan, these being protection and
military support for his quest to free his principality. Gruffud ap
Cynan however, whilst being content to offer the former, did all
that he could to dissuade the prince from pursuing the latter.
Thus Gruffudd ap Rhys settled down into a waiting game with
his northern friends, made bearable only by a vision of
loveliness in the form of Gwenllian. When he had first laid his
eyes on her, he thought they were lying for never had he seen
such perfection. Before him stood a tall, slim but curvaceous
princess adorned in a beautiful full length pale blue silk gown
with large maunch sleeves that followed the contours of her

body like the bark on a tree. Her golden mane was fashioned into two separate plaits, that fell to her hips, each being neatly intertwined by long decorative strands of coloured silk ribbons that provided a perfect visual compliment to her dress. Gwenllian was also understandably drawn to this dashing, ambitious and handsome young prince, who never failed to impress everyone with whom he came into contact. That was, everyone except her wise father, who always managed to keep him at arms length.

The enormous might that Henry had recently assembled against the Welsh had left an open festering wound that turned the once fearless and, some would say, reckless warrior king into a man of caution and apprehension. This would explain Gruffudd ap Cynan's stance towards his regal guest who, despite having to endure frustration, was nevertheless enjoying the kind hospitality afforded by Gwenllian and her family. Angharad grew to admire the young prince as if he were her own son. Gwenllian's brothers on the other hand found a new tutor to share with them the benefits of his considerable knowledge of warfare tactics that, like their father's, had been cultivated among Irish nobles. Gruffudd ap Cynan's elusiveness continued, and when the subject of armed intervention in southern Wales was brought up in court conversation, he would quickly make his excuses and leave. However, he knew that it was only a matter of time before he would have to face the wrath of Henry for providing a 'rebel' with a safe house.

Then, almost on cue, a letter arrived from Henry cordially inviting Gruffudd ap Cynan to London, which the Welsh leader recognised as nothing less than a summons to answer for his befriendment of the renegade prince. For all he knew this summons could cost him far more than the recent urpsing.

Two things were more dear to Gruffudd ap Rhys however than all else, and both rooted him to the house of Gwynedd. On the one hand was his blossoming love for Gwenllian and on the other was the hope that her father would finally relent and provide the support he so desperately desired. What could be described as an uneasy contentment therefore descended on Gruffudd and Gwenllian, with whom he now intimately shared his hopes and fears. Whilst much of their relationship was conducted in full view of the court, privately their passions soared no doubt injected by the excitement of having to fulfil their ardour in secret. Like all young hot blooded couples, the mere fact that the forbidden fruit was there drove them all the more to taste it, and where wisdom once prevailed, emotions now reigned supreme.

The Deheubarth prince's intentions towards Gwenllian would certainly not have escaped her father's notice, who only found it added more and more fuel to the dilemma that he now faced. This was a man torn between his fatherly aspirations for his daughter, whose union with her handsome and patriotic Welsh prince would have filled him with pride, and yet it could undermine the peaceful status quo of the kingdom by attracting the unwanted attention of the fearsome and powerful Norman king. It was this conundrum that scoured the older man's mind as he set out with a handful of his most trusted men, along with a secondary escort of 'fine nobles of England' sent by Henry to ensure his Welsh subordinate's safe arrival in London. As Gruffudd followed the long dusty trail to Henry's court, his unease would have been matched only by the fatigue of the journey itself.

While Gruffudd was away, Hywel ap Rhys, the youngest son of the late Rhys ap Tewdwr, was finally freed from Montgomery Castle. His release was made possible by the substantial influence of his big sister Nest, and not as expected by his now militarily constrained brother. The moving scene when the surviving brothers met for the first time since their separation as children during the tumultuous period after Rhys's calamitous death would not have failed to move Gwenllian and her family. The trials and tribulations endured by both brothers set alight their kindred spirit, creating a new sense of vigour, especially for the older brother. Surely now was the time he had so patiently waited for. The last two clandestine trips to meet the loyal freemen of Deheubarth had brought forth the belief that his people were at last ready. Now with his brother at his side, what could go wrong?

Tentatively breaking the news of his imminent departure to his sweetheart was not easy, because it meant an enforced separation. However, Gwenllian begged that he stay on the side of caution, by remaining just a little longer until her father returned. She sincerely felt sure that her father would also appreciate that a window had opened and would relent by providing the much needed armed assistance.

In London however, the manipulative Norman monarch plied his talents to the full. In the hands of such a devious fox, Gruffudd ap Rhys became more and more pliable. It did not take Henry long to identify Gruffudd's weaknesses. Despite his advancing years, the elderly Welsh leader's libido was not showing any signs of waning, and Henry satisfied his needs by feeding him a convoy of maidens, washed down with copious amounts of his best wine. Compared to the humble surroundings of Aberffraw, Henry's court was luxurious; indeed, this was a classic case of 'seeing how the other half lived'. Like a poacher craftily tickling a blissfully ignorant trout before casting it out onto the bank with sublime skill, Henry now sunk his talons into Gruffudd, who was out of his depth. Having completed the softening-up process, Henry showed his true colours He approached his inebriated guest in a manner previously lacking and pledged unrivalled vengeance on any man who would offer assistance to the renegade Deheubarth princes. On the other hand, Henry stated, should they be captured and delivered to London dead or alive, their captor would receive his life-long protection and gratitude. With a mind awash with alcohol, Gruffudd ap Cynan swore undying loyalty to the Norman king and predicted that he would 'have their heads delivered on a platter' within a week. Unbeknown to either men, a member of the court staff had family links to Gerald de Windsor and overheard their conversation. Without delay, a messenger was sent to Nest in Pembroke warning of the imminent threat to her brothers' lives. Horrified, she despatched her swiftest rider to Gwynedd with the dire news. Her shocked brothers had no choice but to flee the palace, but not before a tearful Gwenllian had persuaded her lover to seek the protection of the church in Aberdaron, whilst she and her family would endeavour to sway the mind of the king from enacting such a terrible deed.

With Gruffudd ap Cynan only a day's ride away, Gruffudd and Hywel ap Rhys made tracks along the Llŷn Peninsula to the little church, still believing that Gwenllian would make her father see sense. However, her pleas fell on deaf ears, for Gruffudd ap Cynan knew that if he was not seen to be fulfilling Henry's explicit instructions, then thousands would be slaughtered and his kingdom and country could be lost forever. He had observed Henry's military might at first hand and knew that he could never match such a force. Henry had purposely arranged displays of his knights on manoeuvres with their latest siege machines and weaponry, knowing that his guest would be so impressed as to never again threaten his control over north Wales. Though it greatly pained him, especially now that he was away from the mesmerising atmosphere of London, he ordered a heavily armed posse to arrest and return the absconding princes to Aberffraw.

Fortunately, when they fled Aberffraw, the two loyal Deheubarth men who had accompanied Gruffudd ap Rhys when he had first arrived in Gwynedd were instructed to seek Nest at Pembroke Castle, delivering a request from her brothers to send a boat to Aberdaron to facilitate their escape. Gruffudd's powerful guard arrived at the picturesque church only to be faced with a resilient and adamant priest who warned of 'hell and damnation descending upon those who break the sanctity of the church!'. Fearing for their very souls, the guards reluctantly withdrew and instead sought further instruction from their king. This gave the young princes the time to board the now waiting boat and head for south Wales. The fact that troops had arrived at the church confirmed that Gwenllian had been unsuccessful in her endeavours, and that certain death awaited them in north Wales. Therefore, as far as they were concerned, their flight from Gwynedd was justified.

The long and sometimes choppy journey to Pembroke lasted a day and a half, and gave Gruffudd ap Rhys time to reflect and plan his next move. His heart grew heavier as the distance increased between him and his sweetheart, but it also burned with the fire of vengeance, which he and his brother would now inflict on all emissaries of Henry throughout south Wales.

CHAPTER FOUR

"LOVE AND WAR"
1116 - 1117

With her lover and his brother now relatively safe in south Wales, Gwenllian could breath a sigh of relief. And rightly so for her father had, uncharacteristically, totally spurned her desperate appeals to spare their lives. Showing none of his usual warmth, the grey and steely-eyed old warrior simply cast her aside, justifying his actions as being 'for the benefit of Gwynedd'.

It was not long however before news reached Aberffraw of the resurgent south Wales prince who had gathered a force of young fellow patriots, all carrying swords of vengeance. The long years of patiently waiting, masking and manacling the thunder that raged in his blood now burst onto Norman, Fleming and Saxons alike, as he and his forces descended like a host of howling banshees.

Operations headquarters were safely tucked away at Caeo in Cantref Mawr, high in the upper reaches of Dyffryn Twyi (valley). It was a place that was described in later years by Geraldus Cambrensis as 'the safest of refuges, because of the tangled density of its forests'.

These impenetrable woodland facades greatly contrasted the neighbouring exposed barren landscape that was carpeted with heather and interrupted only by the odd cluster of bilberry bushes and wiry hawthorn trees. Though naturally adventuristic and patriotic, this band of young partisans were also drawn to the standard of Gruffudd ap Rhys by the notion of acquired wealth through plunder. With winter fast approaching, time was of the essence and so the campaign of terror and ethnic cleansing commenced without delay. Gruffudd was a man who led from the front, no doubt instilled from observing the reckless Irish who still fought in the old way, in pursuit of personal glory rather than as a cohesive unit in the manner of the Normans. This, however, also suited the typically Welsh method of conducting a guerilla form of warfare by ambush, hit and run. Being a host of ferocious individualistic warriors hellbent on murder, they competed for the prize of the greatest number of kills and, as in Roman times, put the fear of God into their enemies.

Down they swept like an avalanche onto the Norman-held fortresses at Llanymddyfri (Llandovery), Narberth, Abertawe (Swansea), Aberteifi (Cardigan) and Aberystwyth. The timber palisade outer defences were no deterrent for the *sons of the dragon*, who tunnelled, climbed and torched their way under, over and through. Once inside, those, who were foolish or brave enough to remain were quickly and efficiently despatched under a hail of thrashing swords, arrows and spears.

It was during this time that an inconsolable yet determined Gwenllian decided that she would elope and join her true love to participate in the struggle in regaining his principality. With the full knowledge and blessing of her family, excluding her unremitting father who showed no signs of changing his stance, she sent a message to Gruffudd ap Rhys explaining her intentions, via the only known channel of communication, his sister Nest. It wasn't long before the reply arrived: 'a ship will collect you at Aberdaron point on the early morning tide in two days. Be there!' It was signed by Nest. Her mother and fellow siblings knew she would be safe, for this was no ordinary princess. Blessed with the looks and grace of a Greek goddess, her spirit and determination cut with the depth of a razor edged sword. Nothing would deter her from this dangerous journey of destiny. Gathering together just a few personal belongings and seasonally appropriate clothing, she bade her secret emotional farewells to family and trusted friends. Her brother Owain, the future Owain Gwynedd, was already the second most powerful person in the kingdom, and offered her his full support by arranging a small armed escort to Aberdaron. By wearing the mantle, leather tunic and trews of a Welsh warrior, she drew less attention than a colourfully garbed princess would have drawn. Gruffudd ap Cynan had taken leave to attend a meeting with local chieftains in his subsidiary palace in Aber, east of Bangor. Therefore, in his absence, a heavy hearted Gwenllian slipped away before dawn to avoid being seen by other court residents.

As they made steady progress along the Llŷn Peninsula, conversation with her escort remained minimal to say the least. Her actions were unprecedented and well she knew it. Indeed, the ramifications of her flight to her lover were incalculable for, as close to her father as she was, she knew that with increasing age his behaviour was becoming increasingly irrational. It was quite possible that she may even trigger an armed response from his powerful Gwynedd forces resulting in the complete annihilation of Gruffudd ap Rhys and his followers.

Despite her fears and doubts, intuitively she drove on for the power of love holds no bounds, even for a Welsh princess normally constrained by and steeped in traditions that demand and impose conformity on those of lesser spirit than herself. It was however ironic that her own father had spurned his own parent's preceptions when he chose to woo, win and wed the beautiful Angharad, instead of seeking a wife amongst the daughters of the reigning princes in Wales at the time.

Safely aboard the vessel that appeared as predicted, Gwenllian sailed to Pembroke Castle. After receiving a warm greeting from Nest and a spending a short period convalescing, she was escorted to the mountain fastness of the anxiously

Chester castle - within these walls Gwenllian's father, Gruffudd was placed 'out of harm's way'.

Abermenai – where Gwenllian's father – Gruffudd ap Cynan first landed after returning from exile in Ireland.

Aberffraw then - birthplace of Gwenllian and historic seat of the rulers of Gwynedd. It is believed that the location of her first home (the king's palace) lies buried beneath the foundations of a housing estate.

Aberffraw – today

The misty outline of the Snowdon range – safe haven to
the Gwynedd royal family.

Pembroke castle – this powerful Norman fortress was home to
Gerald-de-Windsor and his wife Nest, sister of Gruffudd ap Rhys.

Caeo – this basin formed into the side of the hill in medieval times would have been hidden beneath the canopy of the dense forest and, arguably, could have been a possible location for Gwenllian and Gruffudd's hideout.

Caeo - high in the hills of Cantref Mawr, where the remains of the thick deciduous forest still cloak the skyline.

Carmarthen castle – sat at the heart of the epic struggle between Norman and Welsh forces in Deheubarth.

Aberystwyth castle - at nearby Plas Crug, a combined Norman force from Aberystwyth and Ystrad Meurig castles routed Gruffudd ap Rhys and his followers.

Castell Dinefwr – the traditional historic seat of the rulers of Deheubarth, where Gwenllian and her forces slipped quietly by en-route to Cydweli.

Cydweli castle

Cydweli castle - the inner keep of this soon to be infamous fortress, though originally of timber construction, was where Gwenllian resided whilst carrying her first child.

Cydweli castle - this is the location of the original drawbridge and main entrance to the castle. It is here facing the castle ramparts you will find the 'Gwenllian Monument', standing in open defiance to Norman rule.

Llys Rhosyr – a palace of the princes of Gwynedd. Built during the
period of Owain Gwynedd – (Gwenllian's brother).

Mynydd y Garreg – seen here from a distance, where Gwenllian
made her secret encampment with her followers.

Maes Gwenllian – in the foreground, is the actual location where the epic struggle took place. Hidden in the deep grass are a circle of stones said to be where Gwenllian fell.

Battlefield – this is the perspective the Norman knights had from the upper slopes of Mynydd y Garreg.
Also, to the left of the field can be seen 'Gwenllian Farm'.

Cardigan Castle - The sad remains of what was regarded by the Welsh forces as the 'toughest nut to crack'.

Bangor cathedral

Bangor cathedral – somewhere beneath the seating to the right of the alter, lies the remains of Gruffudd ap Cynan along with his wife and sons Owain (Gwynedd) and Cadwaladr.

The Coat of Arms of Gruffudd ap Cynan - described as: *Gules, Three Lioncels Passant in Pale Barry Argent, Armed Azure*. Seen here proudly displayed above the 'Precentor's Stall', in Bangor cathedral. Gwenllian grew up under the protection of this powerful symbol.

Tyddewi, *St David's*, the site of a carved stone effigy of Gwenllian's
son Yr Arglwydd Rhys and his reputed burial place.

GERLLAW Y LLE HWN
YM MAES GWENLLIAN
Y CYNHALIWYD Y SEIAT GYNTAF
GAN Y METHODISTIAID
YN 1741

Dedication to Gwenllian on wall of Methodist church on
Mynydd y Garreg (Church directly overlooks Maes Gwenllian).

Memorial Stone of Yr Arglwydd Rhys - standing at the foot of the ruins of Cardigan Castle, you will see this commemoration to the youngest son of Gwenllian and Gruffudd ap Rhys.

Gwenllian Court Hotel – proudly display her name and have a small memorial to her in the reception area.

Gwenllian Farm – the present owners and custodians of a special place in Welsh history, 'Maes Gwenllian'.

Gwenllian's monument at Cydweli castle – erected by
Merched y Wawr and unveiled by Gwynfor Evans in 1991.

awaiting Gruffudd ap Rhys. He, above all, fully appreciated the tremendous sacrifice made by his lover, to turn her back on her father's expectations and join in unsanctioned union with the man, whom Gruffudd ap Cynan now judged to be his enemy. She found him with his men in a sheltered glacially carved valley in the most inaccessible parts of Ystrad Twyi. Hidden amongst the vast expanse of dense deciduous forest, where Red Kite, Buzzard, Goshawk and Sparrow Hawk jostle for supremacy over territorial boundaries, Gwenllian settled into a humble existence not normally befitting a royal princess. However, this was a war zone that necessitated the sacrifice of life's comforts.

When she arrived, the conditions more resembled livestock accomodation than a potential family home. Therefore, one of her first tasks was to make the inhospitable hospitable. At her insistence an area of the forest was cleared to allow for the construction of a small bower that afforded much warmer, drier and cleaner habitation. The other chicken hut dwellers decided that they too would learn from her example and built similar shelters, thus creating a woodland village that could withstand the harsh winters of the region.

Many of the by now substantial force gathered at Gruffudd ap Rhys's side were not quite sure about the new arrival because they feared that she might take some of the fire out of his avenging sword. However, their fears were soon allayed when she accompanied them to raid a Flemish settlement, acquitting herself as well as any man in the bloody fighting that ensued. These defiant Welshmen were fiercely proud of their ancient heritage and could implicitly recite the details of the great struggle of Buddug (Boudica), whose uncompromising spirit they no doubt saw flickering again in this powerful charismatic princess. Gwenllian's infectious zeal towards the warrior pathway positively galvanised the partisans who quickly accepted her as the mother of the Deheubarth cause. As time progressed the young couple, having long made plain their feelings for each other, found the decision to marry came easily, especially when they considered the practical benefits. With the blessing of the church, more people would be drawn to the cause. In addition, by uniting the bloodlines of Gwynedd and Deheubarth, the threat from her father would lessen if not totally diminish. Once again they turned to Nest for assistance. Nest was delighted for her brother as was Hywel, and she soon made the necessary arrangements for the secret ceremony. Nest was a stunningly beautiful medieval diva who positively reveled in the power of directorship, which she wielded in both Welsh and Norman camps, yet at the same time remaining insular from the obvious dangers of her dualism. This was understandable when you consider the unique status she afforded; on the one side she commanded the undying affection and protection of one of the most powerful Norman lords in south Wales, while on the other she was the sister of a Welsh prince who by now had at his disposal the largest Welsh army that had been assembled in south Wales since the ascendence of their father.

A day of celebration was a welcome relief for the hard pressed forces. The open air ceremony was conducted in front of an audience of literally hundreds, followed by song, dance and the consumption of huge amounts of plundered Norman and Flemish food and beverage. For a short period of time, the hitherto cold and uninviting cathedral vaults that were formed by an avenue of hanging oak trees positively pulsed with the warmth of human merriment. Gwenllian had got her man, and he had secured the lifelong love and support of a beautiful eighteen year old warrior-goddess, who would go on to become the backbone of his struggle against Norman oppression.

When the euphoria of the joyous occasion had lifted and grim reality had returned to sink deep into their consciousness, Gwenllian insisted that she still accompany her new husband on his daring raids, despite his misgivings over her safety. Onward they pressed however, with unparalleled daring and mischief, mainly attacking small targets that gave rich pickings because they were carefully chosen to sap the already waning moral of the occupying forces.

Then came the day when Gruffudd felt confident enough to take on a major Norman establishment in south Wales – Carmarthen Castle in Caerfyrddin. Much to her husband's relief, Gwenllian decided to remain at their mountain hideout on account of the waves of sickness now gripping her body, heralding the fact that she was with child.

They knew that the castle would no be a push-over for, besides its strong Norman garrison, Gruffudd's clergy spies confirmed that it was also defended by local Welsh leaders and their followers who were Norman sympathisers and had sworn to fight their own countrymen should it be attacked. This only fired the passions of the Deheubarth forces to make an example of such traitors. The attack commenced at dusk in late autumn, the best means of access having been previously surveyed. Under the cover of the long shadows cast from a sun slowly disappearing over the horizon, they scaled the high battlements and only made their presence apparent when sufficient numbers had mustered on its ramparts in the darkness. An ear piercing yell shook the bewildered defenders into action and in the intense hand-to-hand combat that followed, the Normans and their Welsh lapdogs were hacked to death by the determined and vengeful marauders, led in person by their heroic prince. The fact that Welshmen had defended foreign-owned property against their own brothers stood testament to the cancerous nature of Norman infiltration tactics. Payment for past favours were called in with sufficient malice and fortitude that potential patriots were turned into traitors.

Whilst the drama inside the castle unfolded, outside in the adjacent town most of the Norman vassals who had not escaped were put to the sword and their homes and businesses burned to the ground. The castle was spared from a fiery end, but was instead stripped to the bone thus decommissioning it from active service. From the notoriety gained after this daring and successful raid, Gruffudd was elevated to celebrity status amongst his own people and to that of a feared devil amongst the Normans and their servants. The mere mention of his name, by those under threat from Norman patrols, would send the protagonists scurrying back behind their high walls in fear for their lives.

Gruffudd went on to storm and capture Cydweli Castle, but purposely left this military abode in good order, for he decided to relocate Gwenllian into the comforts of its keep, which was a blessing for his now heavily pregnant wife. This bold statement was also designed to send a message to Henry, that his grip on south Wales was slipping.

Feeling ever more confident after his meteoric rise, Gruffudd turned his attention to Ceredigion. This was after the local leaders had sent a written deposition requesting his intervention in halting the incoming tide of Norman-driven Flemish and Saxon settlers. He replied in a manner fully befitting a leader riding on the crest of a wave of public support by confirming that he would not only rid them of the settlers but he would also drive out the Norman lords and their vassals.

The people rallied to his standard the moment he crossed the border. With forces swelled by this influx, his initial encounters met with glorious success. His first success was the fortress of the Earl of Striguil at Blaenporth, Gwithian. Despite strong resistance from its defenders, who suffered severe loss of life, it fell in a matter of hours to the overwhelming numbers fielded by Gruffudd. The structure that had once stood proud to represent Norman conquest and control was summarily torched.

This would set a precedent for what he intended to inflict on all other bastions of foreign power throughout the region. Meticulous and careful planning had paved the way to this moral victory, which was celebrated all the more when, at the end of the siege, it was realised that Gruffudd had only lost one patriot compared to the hundred or more killed on the opposing side. As had been done in Deheubarth, Gruffudd redistributed all surplus taxes confiscated from the inner keep of the fortress back to the local people who now looked upon him as their saviour. On marched the jubilant host to their next objective; the infamous Norman defensive settlement in Penweddig. Unfortunately, or fortunately if you happened to be on the other side, the Normans had been warned of the approaching hordes and fled to the coast to shelter behind the substantial walls of Cardigan Castle in Aberteifi.

Still clear in his objectives, Gruffudd drove the vanguard on to a fortress called Ystrad Peithyll in northern Ceredigion, owned by the steward of the Earl of Striguil. The momentum of this vast Welsh army had created yet another bow wave-like killing zone that saw the complete annihilation of the pitiful garrison that had been ordered to stand fast. This was a wild-fire of freedom fed by the venting spleens of these Welsh equalisers, who fervently believed that they could see for the first time a glimmer of light at the end of the long dark tunnel of Norman tyranny. With confidence abounding, they moved on Aberystwyth Castle with its substantial garrison, an objective that Gruffudd knew would not be an easy nut to crack. He therefore decided to rest his battle weary forces before making his move, a hesitance which though commendable at face value, unfortunately proved to be a fatal mistake that would later cost him dearly. They set up camp at Plas Crug, within shouting distance of the castle and in full view of its inhabitants. This was in complete contradiction to what any successful general or warlord would recommend, that you should never let your enemy see the full extent of your forces, but instead always leave them guessing as to where they are located and the total number of men fielded.

Gruffudd not only showed the watching Normans his full hand, but he also gave them time to call reinforcements from the castle at nearby Ystrad Meurig. These rushed to the rescue and, in a pincer like manoeuvre involving troops from Aberystwyth Castle, jointly smashed into the unprepared and resting Welsh. Despite making a brave stand, the Welsh foot soldiers stood little chance against the advancing heavy cavalry, who swept down on them after a host of archers hidden in a nearby wood had already wreaked havoc. During the general rout, the Deheubarth prince only narrowly escaped with his life, fleeing to the only place where he knew he was safe – the mountains.

Back in Cydweli, tucked up snug and warm in the soft, inviting furnishings of the keep, Gwenllian was lost in her thoughts. She had been dreaming of a morning when she could wake up to be greeted by an end to all hostilities. Just to be able to live in peace with her husband and future child or children in a land bathed in the light of security and love would be a dream come true. But then the harshness of reality rose its ugly head and jolted her back to earth with a bump. From the lips of an exhausted horseman who had ridden non-stop from the horrific scenes at Aberystwyth, she heard of the disaster. Without a moment to lose, she gathered her belongings and returned to Cantref Mawr with her hopes and aspirations in tatters. After a tearful and restless night within the dark, damp wattle and daub plastered walls of the secluded pauper's palace, she greeted her bloodstained husband who arrived with an escort of a mere dozen loyal men. This was in sharp and shocking contrast to the near thousand strong army that had left only a few weeks earlier. His pain was legibly etched on his face for, besides losing his grip on Deheubarth, he had also seen his brother slain at his side.

CHAPTER FIVE

"FUGITIVES"
1117 - 1127

Realising how desperate his situation was, Gruffudd insisted that Gwenllian should take flight to a safe house whilst he continued the struggle from his forest hideaway. This was a wise move for Gwenllian soon gave birth to a son. He was born free, in a place protected by loyal people. The boy was called Anarawd, heir to the most precarious crown in the whole of the long fabled isles of Britain.

Though his secluded forest home had served the purpose in the past, by virtue of its inaccessibility, it seems that Gruffudd's judgement to return there so as to continue the fight was ill-conceived on this occasion. Henry I rejoiced with the news that Norman forces had repelled and broken the Welsh army and therefore decided to strike whilst the iron was hot by ordering the turn-coat, Owen ap Cadwgan, to assemble sufficient men at arms to 'destroy the remnants of the Deheubarth insurgence'. At the same time, he sent orders to Gerald de Windsor to 'strike from the south'.

With a substantial detachment of loyal Powys troops, and a promise of Norman gold for their efforts, it did not take Owen long to locate and throw a secure cordon around Gruffudd's forest hideout. With the noose gradually tightening, the distraught and furious prince decided, with the support of his men, to make a break for it and fight their way out. Peering out from the undergrowth at the ring of mounted assassins that had formed a human chain, they quickly located where the line was at its weakest and charged into the fray, in a cavalry arrowhead formation designed to smash their way through its perimeter. In the melee that followed, Gruffudd escaped, but lost half his men in the process, prompting a furious Owen who, having allowed the target of his exertions slip through his fingers, to gratuitously torch and destroy all the dwellings of the rebel prince before embarking on a systematic search of the surrounding countryside. Unbeknown to Owen ap Cadwgan however, and surely he deserved everything coming to him, his nemesis in the form of Gerald de Windsor was fast approaching with a large Anglo/Norman/Flemish force. In what can only be described as 'pre-meditated payback', Gerald took the opportunity to avenge himself on the man who had deeply humiliated him by kidnapping his beloved Nest.

One can not help but ponder on the distinct probability that Henry and Gerald conspired to rid themselves of two baleful influences in this one single action. Owen ap Cadwgan was genuinely surprised to encounter Gerald's troops in this mountain location, but Gerald on the other hand was fully prepared for and expected to face the dissident Welsh troops. When the two forces met, confusion reigned amidst the Welsh whilst on the other side there was total and absolute cold-blooded certainty. Owen did his best to repel the attack, but eventually fell pierced by half a quiver-full of arrows.

Thus ended the life of the dashing prince of Powys who had the potential to rival any legendary Welsh hero but whose ascending light soon dimmed the day he entered into a pact with a single minded and immoral foreign king.

The one glimmer of hope that emerged during this dreadful time was that Gwenllian's father had formally agreed to cease his feudal intentions towards his new son-in-law. This left the door open for the support and protection they so desperately needed, especially now that their compatriots had deserted them, along with their good fortunes. Though events had effectively made the warrior prince and princess impotent, in militarily terms, the next few years, despite being forced to constantly stay one step ahead of the assassins blade, proved that even the pragmatic Henry could not hold their passions in check, for a further two sons were born. First came Morgan in 1118 and then Maelgwn in 1120 entered the world to be greeted by their aunts, uncles and grandparents after Gwenllian was persuaded to accept their secret protective custody in Aberffraw. Her return to the bosom of her Gwynedd family was greatly assisted by Henry's continued policy of leaving the Welsh kingdom in peace to prosper under Gruffudd ap Cynan. This astute act was paying handsome dividends, for not only did Henry prosper from the heavy tribute collected annually, but so too did the Welsh leader who also saw his military power base and personal wealth grow year by year.

The die, however, had been cast that would set the pattern of the lives of the now fugitive prince and princess. In heavy disguise they continued to move from safe house to safe house only returning to Aberffraw as a respite from their arduous existence. The misery of those wilderness years, especially for a young mother and loyal wife, is beyond comprehension. Her unflinching belief of better times ahead however kept her and her despondent husband going.

Fear of assassination followed them like a bad smell twenty-four hours a day year in, year out. Henry's poisonous tentacles could reach into the very heart of Wales, and well they knew it. It would only be a matter of time before those who had sworn undying loyalty to the cause and in whose hands they were now forced to place their lives turned the royal couple in or murdered them, out of fear for their own safety or the attraction of receiving the substantial bounty placed on their guests heads.

Meanwhile, during 1121 in Powys, the seeds of discontent were once again sprouting when the late Owen ap Cadwgan's uncle Maredudd ap Bleddyn, along with three of Owen's surviving bothers, rose in open revolt against Norman occupation. Gruffudd ap Rhys understandably stayed aloof from this insurrection. His affection for the sons of Powys was far from cordial after their abortive attempt on his life and he decided to leave well alone, allowing Henry's customary response to run its course.

Almost on cue in the summer of that year, from his base in Chester, Henry invaded Wales for a second time. The rabbits he now sought for the pot excluded Gruffudd ap Cynan of Gwynedd and Gruffudd ap Rhys of Deheubarth. As Henry entered Powys at the head of a mighty force, Maredudd and his nephews had carefully planned his assassination by ordering a large group of young reckless longbowmen to 'unleash hell's missiles upon his person' as soon as he came within range. They nearly succeeded for were it not for his breastplate, an arrow would have pierced his heart. The shock of this close, albeit failed attempt, forced Henry to immediately pull back his forces to a safer location from where he sent an ultimatum to Maredudd to pay tribute or die. Maredudd considered his options and soon realised that he did not stand a chance against the overwhelming numbers of troops brought to the field by Henry. He accepted Henry's 'impossible to fulfil' fine of ten thousand cattle, which the astute Norman king knew Maredudd would never be able to pay and would therefore forever be in his debt and left beholding to his pleasure.

Gruffudd ap Rhys's decision to remain neutral throughout the latest Norman – Welsh skirmishes endeared him to Henry's favour. As a reward, the threat of hostile intensions against Gruffudd and Gwenllian was removed, granting them rights to return to a life of relative normality, subject however to certain conditions. They had to live in a chosen location under Norman control and swear to withdraw from all future violent conduct against Henry's crown. Though not exactly impressed by this 'generous' offer, Gruffudd ap Rhys reluctantly accepted his terms, but kept his fingers crossed when it came to the withdrawal of future violence.

Gruffudd did not immediately realise that he was effectively fettered and under house arrest, marshalled by Norman nobles living close by. But even this was better than the constant threat to his family when on the run. For Gruffudd ap Rhys was no different from other men of decent intensions in respect of his family's needs. He desired the best of everything for his wife and children. He may even have thought that, by acting in good faith to Henry's partial amnesty, albeit on the surface, he may endear himself to such an extent that ultimately some of his princely rights over Deheubarth might be returned.

Living amongst Henry's lesser nobles in the newly rebuilt settlments near Carmarthen Castle in Caerfyrddin was not exactly the perfect environment Gwenllian had in mind to bring up her children. Daily her sons faced taunts and sometimes beatings from their Norman born peers. However, when their parents ventured outside the boundary of the prison-like home, no one would dare raise a hand against them without risking a quick and painful release from mother earth.

A further three years of undignified existence under the Norman microscope was unbearable for the free spirited couple. Their accommodation, though basic, was sufficient enough to provide protection from the ravages of the notorious Welsh winters, but even so it seems to have had a detrimental affect on their passions. Whether a conscious decision or the result of the imposed stresses of being under house arrest, but no child was conceived during this depressing period.

They were however, able to keep abreast of evolving situations outside their encapsulated world through maintaining contact with Welsh clergy. A glimmer of hope reached the couple in 1124 with the news of Gwenllian's brother's awakening in response to unsavoury manoeuvres by Maredudd ap Bleddyn. Owain and Cadwaladr had forcibly wrested Meirionnydd from his grasp after he had only recently taken it by force in the first place. This came only three years after Maredudd's indignant climb-down at the hands of a vexed and vengeful Henry I. The priesthood were able to feed weekly reports to Gwenllian and Gruffudd via the well established network of churches throughout Wales. News also came from clandestine meetings held with patriotic local leaders who, despite being under Norman scrutiny, kept the shackled couple's revolutionary spirits alive. Eventually in 1127, the friction that had existed between the Norman overlords and their captive guests boiled over. Gruffudd was told of a plan, hatched by their overseers, to write to Henry complaining in the strongest terms that Gruffudd and Gwenllian were once again conspiring and planning treacherous insurgence against his subjects. Their Norman neighbours' actions were born out of bitterness and spite against the so-called *Welsh enemy*, despite the fact that it was they who were the true 'cuckoos in the song-birds nest'.

Gruffudd knew well that this was all Henry needed to order their immediate and forceful transfer to London to stand trial for treason. In this way, Henry's Norman agents in this corner of Wales could remove the targets of their condemnation and hatred from their midst forever.

Gruffudd, Gwenllian and their children slipped out in the dead of night with wings on their heels, and headed once again for their mountain fastness in Cantref Mawr. There, amongst the dense wooded wilderness, they took shelter under its leafy canopy, initially sitting amongst the charred remains of the late Owen ap Cadwgan's handiwork. Wisely however, with the help of family and a small band of loyal friends, a new and safer site was located where adequate dwellings were soon erected. Here was their new home, from where they would strategize to bring some reality to the deceitful accusations that were made to the Norman king. They, like their new neighbours the wild wolf and hawk, preyed on the abundant forest resources to survive, and with the same spirit and vigour that these powerful and

cunning beasts applied to ensnare their quarry, they would like-
wise stalk the Normans and their collaborators.

CHAPTER SIX

"TIME TO REBUILD"
1127 - 1135

With the taste of freedom returning to their parched lips, they drank fully of its pleasures. Now unshackled from the prying eyes of unfriendly neighbours, they once again breathed the fragrant scented air of a wild Welsh forest. Hunting for food, though a necessity, became a unified family pastime. They were like birds re-learning the beauty of flight after years of having clipped wings.

News of their escape from Caerfyrddin spread throughout Wales and it was not long before another ripple of brave *Cymry* gathered at Cantref Mawr. However, the harsh realisation that years of enforced leave had waned the patriotic passions of their subjects soon became apparent when no more than fifty warriors assembled at their side.

While Gruffudd ap Rhys and his limited war band harassed the enemy, Gwenllian busied herself instructing her sons in the fighting arts in which she had long excelled. This was the first opportunity in years to wield a sword, thrust a lance or shoot an arrow with malice, and she found it to be positively refreshing. The bearing of arms in Caerfyrddin had been strictly forbidden under the draconian conditions laid down by Henry. Against timber posts driven deep into the ground and standing the height of a full grown man, they trained with swords and shields to simulate inflicting wounds on Norman flesh. This precious time spent learning the warrior ways would become essential to assist them in their future struggles against the harsh times that fate would inevitably throw at them. Now in her thirtieth year, Gwenllian wore borrowed rags and took on a gypsy-like appearance, but still retained the regal air that instilled respect from all who ventured into her home. Due to the lack of physical and material resources, successful raids were few and far between. Yet on they drove, relentless in their convictions that they were fighting to keep alive the spirit of freedom.

The seasons came and went and months turned into years. Conditions were hard, but the knowledge that they were now living on free Welsh soil was adequate compensation. During lulls in the fighting, Gwenllian and her sons under small escort would journey to Aberffraw for family reunions and, despite their pleas for her to remain under Gwynedd protection, she was steadfast in her heart that her place was at her husband's side rather than cowering in the shadows of her parents' palace. Just when things seemed to be mildly improving, in 1132 Gwenllian received the tragic news that her youngest brother, Cadwallon, had been ambushed and killed whilst raiding Norman and Powys positions in Nanheudwy (near Llangollen). After bitter hand-to-hand fighting he was captured, immediately sentenced and summarily executed.

Then during 1133, Gwenllian gave birth to what would be her last child; it seems that the couple were fated only to produce sons, though she dearly wished for a daughter. However, this child would be special, eclipsing his brothers in much the same way that Gwenllian had her siblings. Through trials and tribulations, he would rise from the ashes of his ancestors to become known as *yr Arglwydd Rhys* (the Lord Rhys).

A unique situation was evolving however in the struggle to

recover Deheubarth. Gruffudd ap Rhys seemed to be in an enviable position in that he could turn the tap of aggression on or off as it pleased him. Henry's troops now no longer pursued their quarry to the ends of what earth they knew, although they still fought to keep control over unlawfully seized Welsh property or land. It appears their policy seemed to be shifting to that of consolidation rather than expansionism, as was the norm for those of Viking blood.

Despite the lack of fervour in the Norman camp, Gruffudd was unable to take full advantage of what seemed like a golden opportunity to recover his lost lands. Just as the Romans had succeeded in doing a millennium earlier, the Normans applied the same methods of pacification on the native population. Intermarital agreements between the sons and daughters of Norman and Welsh nobles were actively promoted, although to the majority of Welsh nationalists just the idea was repulsive. There were, however, the usual treacherous dogs of war, who cared less for the future of their country than what riches it could provide them.

The advent of this general malaise was effectively nullifying the feudal landscape of Wales. The welcome news of Henry's demise in France came as a beam into the general gloom however. The much feared and, to a lesser degree, respected monarch had died while staying in winter lodgings on a hunting trip near Lyons. Like all supreme rulers who answer to no one but the Almighty or their conscience, he decided that he knew more than his learned physicians who had strongly advised him not to partake in the consumption of Lampreys, an eel-like dish that they had already established as carrying potentially fatal toxins. He discovered to his infinite folly that *doctor knows best*.

Henry's legacy in Wales left all lands east of Afon Clwyd under Norman control while Powys remained a puppet state, lacking strong direction or leadership. Gwynedd continued to prosper and no Norman-held castles blighted its soil, but the southern part of the country moved ever-closer to total Norman domination. At the time of Henry's death, an unusual natural occurrence happened in mid Wales. A huge storm arose, causing lakes and reservoirs to burst their banks and, uncannily in one incident, a pool emptied its complete contents including fish into an adjacent valley. Collectively, the superstitious people saw all this as a sign of great importance, heralding a time of change. Some were even convinced that the legendary hero of Welsh lore, Arthur, was returning as promised to wreak vengeance on all alien souls on Welsh soil. The equally superstitious Flemings immediately sold-up and left Wales in droves, fearful of the repercussions now that their late lord and protector had left them exposed.

The stunned silence that had descended upon Wales, prophetically like the quiet before the storm, was soon replaced by a hum that travelled the length and breadth of the land. The red dragon was drawing in its breath. Meanwhile, in France, carefully laid plans were contrived on the event of the king's death, and were activated with expeditious vigour by Henry's nephew Stephen. With the assistance of lords on both sides of the English channel who had something to gain, he rushed to London to claim the crown despite having sworn an oath nine years earlier to Henry that he would accept the succession of Henry's daughter Matilda in the event of Henry's death.

Concurrent with his deceitful snatching of the English crown, sufficient numbers of nobles in Normandy saw to it that he was recognised and appointed as the Duke of Normandy, thus mirroring the titles of the late king. However, all was not plain sailing for the new king on the northern side of the channel. Robert, Earl of Glamorgan, led the Marcher lords in refusing to acknowledge Stephen as the rightful heir, instead proclaiming their allegiance to Matilda, Robert's half sister. Stephen was no match for the astute Henry in the subtleties of kingdom management, which was well summarised by a chronicler of the time when he described Stephen as 'a good knight, but in all other respects, a fool'.

Amidst the near state of anarchy that existed in England, the Welsh dragon finally spread its wings and took to the air. South Wales was particularly volatile, reflecting the imminence of complete Norman subjugation in the region, compared to that of their lesser-threatened northern brothers. What was regarded as the pivotal action of the latest uprising took place in Penlle'r-gaer, a short distance north of Swansea. A local leader named Hywel ap Maredudd raised a large force to pay back in kind for the harsh treatment that the local Norman occupiers had inflicted upon his countrymen. Despite being faced with combined Norman, Saxon and Flemish troops far greater in number than his own, he secured a resounding victory. The majestic sight of Welsh warriors in full flight as they crashed fearlessly into the ranks of the foe, driven by blood infused with the dragon's spirit, was awe-inspiring. That part of the country had not seen such carnage for decades. On the battlefield lay more than five-hundred enemy dead, and from this triumphant masterstroke the whole nation drew strength.

CHAPTER SEVEN

"MAES GWENLLIAN"
1136

Of all the Norman lords stationed in South Wales, one in particular was destined to collide head-on with Gwenllian. *Maurice de Londres* (Maurice of London) in 1130 took up occupancy of Cydweli Castle and brought with him a demeanour without equal even amongst his own kind.

He soon set about establishing a network of paid native collaborators to assist him in identifying the source of the most likely threat to his rapidly expanding mini-kingdom. With the aid and advice of a local leader named Gruffudd ap Llewelyn, Maurice soon identified the relatively dormant prince and princess of Deheubarth as the most aggressively inclined of Welsh patriots to threaten his domain. There were none who could match the many forays launched by Gruffudd against Norman held Cydweli and the surrounding urban vassal populous over the past eight years.

Meanwhile Gruffudd ap Rhys had been observing and considering the mood of his people in the light of the recent events and firmly came to believe as did many others throughout the country, that the time was ripe for the Normans to bleed. Even though his own forces had swollen in recent days to over five-hundred men-at-arms, he still felt it prudent to call for armed assistance from his father-in-law to ensure maximum

the enemy. Gwenllian also sensed that this was a
ime and wrote a personal letter to her father who,
h blind in old age, still possessed his hearing with which
to ... r its message:

*'Dearest father and mighty king, to demonstrate the sincerity of our
request, my husband makes personal attendance upon your court
and I beseech you to consider carefully his intentions.'*

After much consideration, it was decided that the oldest and
youngest sons, Anarawd and Rhys, would accompany
Gruffudd ap Rhys to Aberffraw, leaving Maelgwn and Morgan
to watch their mother's back amongst the numerous rivals
encamped in and around their home. The bonds of love that
created this unbreakable family unit sprung from the heart of
Gwenllian, and to part company during times when marauding
bandits roamed the hills and assassins plied their wicked trade
was always a tearful and worrying affair. However, as Gruffudd
and his sons prepared to leave, the usual affection openly
displayed between the close-knit family was noticeably tinged
with emotional and contemplative silence for fear of the
unspeakable.

Norman spies plainly resided amongst the Welsh, but so too
did Welsh spies infiltrate the ranks of the Normans. It was from
this source that word came to Gwenllian of Maurice de
Londres's *final solution* intentions towards herself and her
family. He had decided to rid himself of their presence once and
for all, especially once their sporadic but effective raids had
gone beyond a level that could be merely described as a
nuisance. Their threat was having a negative affect on attracting
the money-bearing bursers to his enclave and, as greed for
power and riches featured highly on his agenda, something had
to be done.

His garrison, though strong enough to withstand assaults
from the unfriendly natives, was in no way capable of

successfully mounting a truly destructive Gruffudd ap Rhys's mountain fastness. Mau negotiated with the English crown for a conce dispatch of a substantial task force to be transporte to disembark on the western Glamorgan coast so with his own forces. This at least is what he intende[d] ...enllian to believe. In reality the Normans knew the purpose for Gruffudd ap Rhys's visit to Gwynedd and the dangers to themselves if he succeeded in gaing support from the north. Their policy was simple at least in theory: they intended to disrupt, confuse and disperse the swarm of bees you need to support the queen. Yes, Gwenllian was the target, and they needed to lure her out into the open. This was achieved by feeding distorted facts to the Welsh spies that would give Gwenllian little choice other than to attempt a pre-emptive strike to nullify the threat that Maurice de Londres posed to her family.

An anxious Gwenllian paced the dusty compacted mud floor of her home, considering her options. Should she send a fast rider after her husband and await his return before acting? Or should she unleash with immediate effect her own army, thus gaining the essential element of surprise. She unfortunately chose the latter option having first establishing that each individual captain in her ranks, along with their respective followers, would accept her as their undisputed leader for the campaign ahead.

The answer came swiftly, as the gathered host roared their approval by chanting her name – *Gwenllian! Gwenllian! Gwenllian!* Each captain in turn presented themselves to her on bended knee swearing undying loyalty to in the best chivalric tradition. For how could they deny Gwenllian 'the warrior princess' whose name had now become a byword amongst her own people and, to some, was already a living legend.

The fighting spirits of her loyal followers rose to fever pitch after she had delivered a rousing speech, assuring them that will not rest until every last Norman, Flemish and Saxon is expelled from our mother country'. Appreciating the enormity of the role she was now undertaking, she clad herself in full military regalia comprising mainly of a mail *hauberk* split up the front and rear and terminating just above the knee, under which she neatly tucked her long flowing plaits. On her head she placed a hood of chainmail, known as a *coif-de-mailles*, whilst over the top of these gladiatorial garbs she wore a crimson dyed calf length surcoat. With her kite shaped shield swinging on her back and scabbarded battle sword on her hip she looked every inch the Amazonian queen, or second Penthesileia as *Geraldus Cambrensis* described her in later years. Under cover of darkness, she rode at the head of a great column of men with her sons Maelgwn and Morgan ensconced at her side.

The large force of Welsh heroes comprising of cavalry, foot soldiers and archers, followed a predetermined route intended to cloak their approach to Cydweli Castle. They strictly adhered to the plans previously agreed with her officers that entailed splitting the army in two. One half led by Gwenllian would make their way to a secluded spot at the foot of Mynydd y Garreg, within one mile or less than two kilometers of the castle, while the other group led by her most trusted captain would intercept the Norman reinforcements before they could join up with Maurice de Londres' garrison. When that force had been wiped out, they would rejoin her to secure victory at the castle.

Down Dyffryn Twyi they marched passing through Dinefwr, the traditional seat of the kings of south Wales and in particular Hywel Dda. Although the hill fort ruins were not visible in the ebony shadow of mother earth, it was a poignant reminder as to the justification of their crusade. As they slipped gracefully by the haunting ruins that towered above their heads, Gwenllian turned to her sons and told them of her fervent hope that, one day, she and their father would rebuild Castell Dinefwr to appease the spirits of their ancestors

On they trekked making a wide birth of the settlements of

Llandeilo and especially Caerfyrddin to avoid the prying eyes of enemy informants, who were known to operate in those townships. At Llandyfaelog her army split in two and through stealth and an intricate knowledge of the vast countryside, Gwenllian arrived a few hours before dawn with her now depleted force at the foot of Mynydd y Garreg, only a short distance from their final objective. And there she waited until the cock crowed to herald her attack on the castle.

As dawn approached, she mingled amongst her valiant comrades, openly reciting the plan of attack so that none were left with any doubt as to what was expected of them. This was the first major action sixteen year old Maelgwn and eighteen year old Morgan would experience, a fact the young princes well understood, for their stomaches knotted up in gradients as the hour of attack approached.

Throughout the ranks, however, confidence abounded and the will to press home the attack on their enemies grew as hard as the granite of Mynydd y Garreg itself, that majestically rose like a fortress battlement, guarding their rear and offering reassurance, or at least so they thought. It appears that the trap hatched between Maurice de Londres and his newly appointed first lieutenant, Gruffudd ap Llewellyn was coming together like a finely stitched quilt. For now a tragedy was unfolding, creating its own momentum that nothing could stop. The web of lies, so accurately spun by this dastardly pair, cloaked the cold facts of their sordid plot, which included arranging for the Norman reinforcements to arrive a day earlier than stated. Led by the Welsh traitor and armed with the knowledge of Gwenllian's whereabouts, they had hidden themselves in the misty heights of Mynydd y Garreg overlooking her camp.

Twice the numbers fielded by Gwenllian of ambushers poured down on the unsuspecting encampment in an avalanche of men, swords, shields, spears and battle axes, supported by a hail of deadly arrows from the numerous bowmen hidden amongst the hillside thickets. The initial shock of seeing hordes of heavily armed, chainmail-clad, Normans descending upon them caused men and horses to scatter in all directions. However, Gwenllian, aided by her sons and officers, quickly regrouped her forces to form a shield-wall just as the first wave slammed into them. The attackers were the seasoned shock troops of Normandy, hardened to war and its torrid ways on the unforgiving fields of France. But this would be no push-over, for these devils were on foreign soil and fought only for the incentive of financial and material wealth, while the men who stood fast before them were the Cymry who belonged to the very land on which they fought. With every sinew straining, the Welsh met the foe head-on, roaring like a pride of lions and if death would take them, then so be it for they would gladly die with sword in hand whilst defending their freedom. Gwenllian and her sons were not rushed to safety from the ensuing carnage that by now was being inflicted on both side. To the contrary, they were located in the hub of the battle lines where heroes and heroines are born.

Keeping a safe distance from the cutting edges of Welsh steel, the traitor Gruffudd ap Llewellyn moved freely amongst the French troops, barking out commands and assuring them that the person who killed the rebel princess would receive a generous reward in gold coins. This galvanised the French to spearhead their attack directly at Gwenllian's location. With a mighty thrust of their huge shoulders, behind their curved kite shaped shields, they burst through the Welsh interlocked shield-wall, allowing half a dozen of them to close in on the princess and her sons. Both her sons now frantically fought to hold back the blows directed at their mother. Under such a storm, their once dependable shields slowly disintegrated, and this was the time that the unprotected Maelgwn received the injuries that took his life. Gwenllian immediately let out a shriek that only a mother could express on seeing her son cut down in her defence. The painful and heartbreaking moment of Maelgwn's death only fired her even more as she skilfully applied her sword to deliver death with consummate ease. This unique blend of ferocity and efficiency is only made possible when warrior and weapon are forged into one inseparable unit. With her heavily outnumbered troops stretched to the limit and with their backs to Afon Gwendraeth, no one could rush to her aid, so therefore, for what felt like an eternity, she and her surviving son Morgan stood their ground in a savage exchange of bitter hand-to-hand fighting, intent on taking as many of their attackers with them to the spirit world as possible. It was during this frantic altercation that the valiant princess was struck in the upper arm with the sharp edge of a French sword that completely knocked her off her feet. Morgan unselfishly threw himself between his mother and the beast who was now drawing back his sword to issue the *coup de grâce*, and received the blow to his own side through his unselfish valour. Somehow, thankfully, Gwenllian's dwindling supporters managed to reform and place a cordon around her after they had despatched her immediate threat with enviable efficiency.

With their princess at the centre of a screen of some fifty remaining heroes, they girded their loins to fight with honour to the last, as indeed had their brothers-in-arms who lay strewn about them. Now under attack from all sides, their spirits grew a little when they realised that the French troop's onslaught was showing signs of faltering. However, that all changed when they caught sight of Baron Maurice de Londres at the head of approximately fifty horsemen brashly charging with lances couched under their arms and heading directly towards their defence wall. Smashing into the ring of Welsh muscle, the apocalyptic horsemen killed at least another dozen defenders in the process. Finally, with their spirits broken, the survivors realised all was lost and dropped their arms as a sign of capitulation. However, Gwenllian was quite oblivious to this abrupt ending to the hostilities, as she had been too engrossed in nursing her badly injured son, as one would expect from a desperate mother of renowned compassion. As two burly

Norman knights approached her on foot to secure her arrest, she turned to face them with wild bloodshot eyes, still swollen from the torrent of tears that she had shed for her murdered and injured sons. Then realising all was lost she graciously accepted defeat and took centre stage in the drastic and dreaded performance that followed. The scene where this epic struggle had taken place was illuminated by the soft dawn sunlight now pouring over Mynydd y Garreg's misty undulating horizon. Her contrasting audience was made up by a handful of exhausted and demoralised countrymen, and jeering, elated Normans, each and every one of them settled into an uneasy silence as they awaited judgement on her fate. It was not long in coming; Maurice de Londres spoke in a low tone to his Welsh lieutenant, thankfully inaudible to Gwenllian, for he had just ordered her immediate execution. She was dragged out, hands tethered and forced to stand in front of the Norman puppet traitor who informed her in her native tongue, 'for your crimes against the English crown, you, Gwenllian wife of the rebel Gruffudd ap Rhys, shall receive swift justice at the hands of our finest swordsman'. The unholy words spouted from the bitter and twisted mouth of a professional slayer. This came as a terrible shock to her heavily guarded men, now joined by the injured Morgan who was bearly able to stand. Their disbelief and horror at this judgement was painfully evident, as they vainly attempted to rush to her side to extricate her from this unlawful and terrible ending. Removing her chainmail hood, they drew out her long blonde plaits from under her blood stained hauberk. The solemn and stony silence was interrupted only by her silky surcoat, that now rippled gently in the estuarine breeze, which snaked its way along the contours of the ever-flowing Afon Gwendraeth. Gwenllian acknowledged her fate with a consenting nod, after first spitting in the face of the Welsh traitor who stood before her.

Then turning to her distraught son and followers she shouted, 'Morgan my son, my heart, you and your brave

knights must swear to live on, to tell our pec
here this day'. Then a huge chainmail-clac
forward with broadsword unsheathed. Sh
seconds away from the inevitable when she l
to her son and proclaimed with a voice seared
the knowledge that never again would sh
husband's embrace or caress her beloved son
moments I send my undying love to you, yc .ather and
brothers'. With tears cascading down his flushed and bloodstained cheeks, young Morgan could only nod a response, for he
was too choked to talk.

The two soldiers that had flanked her now separated. One
gathered her long plaited mane and twined it until it took on a
single rope-like appearance and then stood facing her, whilst
the other one positioned himself behind her and held both of
her arms tightly in his grip. With a tug from the front, she was
forced to bend at the hips, exposing the milky white smooth
skin of her neck. Her executioner now stood at her side and
looked to the smirking face of his lord for the command to end
her life. With the same nonchalant tilt of his head that would
grant someone leave from his dining table, he gave the waiting
swordsman his consent. Slowly, the visibly nervous Norman
raised the heavy sword above his head and with one hand on
the hilt and the other on the pommel, he drew in a deep breath
charging energy into his huge arms. But, just a split second
before the razor edge reached its target, a final cry escaped from
Gwenllian's lips that, although its reverberation only reached
the ears of the immediate witnesses, its defiant message would
ultimately be heard throughout the whole of her beloved
Cymru. Two words came from a heart still beating with purity,
light and patriotism.

'Remember Me!' was her cry – and then there was silence.

The Norman soldier, who had taken her life, shook the blade
violently so as to remove her blood and then walked some
distance away, before sinking to his knees, where he wept

...ly whilst praying to God for forgiveness. He knew ...extinguished the light of no mere mortal; this was a ...cess of renowned beauty and bravery. Although she bled ...ke others, he could not help but be moved by the unselfish love and defiance that had poured forth from her very being at a time when you would expect a cry for mercy. A stony-face Morgan and the remnants of her army were led away to a life of incarceration in some filthy rat infested jail or, if their skills were of some use to their Norman overlords, some would die in the ranks of a forlorn regiment on the battle-torn fields of France.

So died a valiant and virtuous princess, whose love for her country was matched only by her love for her family. In addition to her demise, a further five-hundred souls of Norman and Welsh origin lay torn and battered on the field of conflict that day, and those not taken away for honourable burial were left for the crows to feast upon. In the days, weeks and months that followed, Welsh people, including relatives of those killed, came from miles around to discretely pay their respects to their fallen countrymen and loved ones. To this day, the field of glory and tragedy where the flower of Wales met her maker, carries the name *Maes Gwenllian* (Gwenllian's field) for posterity. And nearby, a simple stone monument, erected nearly nine hundred years after her death, stands defiantly facing the main entrance to Cydweli Castle in solemn remembrance of Wales's last warrior-princess.

CHAPTER EIGHT

"AFTERMATH"
1136 - 1200

Whilst hell on earth existed in Cydweli, scenes of merriment resounded in Aberffraw, where peace had prevailed long enough for Gwynedd to have blossomed into a land of fruitful orchards and fair gardens, and especially the green pastures of Arfon and rich meadows of Ynys Môn had won the admiration of folk from far and wide. Gwenllian's husband had like-wise won over the hearts and minds of his in-laws to join his campaign in driving the Normans out of Wales and, therefore, frantic preparations for the invasion of Norman held territories were under way, when an exhausted and weatherbeaten rider approached the royal enclosure.

The fatigued Welshman was helped into the main hall to state his business to the assembled leaders, who were mulling over a parchment discussing strategy of attack. He broke the news in a voice wracked with high emotion and exhaustion. A stunned silence descended upon the hall as they listened intently to the harrowing details. Disbelief was soon followed by a wailing that came from her blood family. Gruffudd ap Rhys and Anarawd sank to their knees with arms around each other trying in vain to offer mutual comfort. Tears and calls for bloody vengeance flowed freely from all gathered in the hall of sorrow.

Gruffudd ap Cynan received the news in his bed chamber,

where he spent most of his time in quiet contemplation, now blind and with a body failing him in degrees. He asked to be left alone in undisturbed reminiscence of his favourite daughter's tumultuous life. His wife however, was inconsolable and openly displayed her grief for the child that had brought such joy into her life, especially during times when depression had haunted her mind. It took two whole days before the war meeting could be reconvened, but now in a far more sombre atmosphere.

Gwenllian's distraught husband and eldest son had left the day before, accompanied by a substantial guard, swelled in numbers by Gwynedd troops provided by his father-in-law. Young Rhys stayed behind under the watchful eyes of a grandmother who doted on the last born of Gwenllian's brood. As the royal widower sank deep into his saddle feeling like he had been torn apart, his mind swam with his first priority when arriving home; to find and recover the bodies of his wife and son and then to pursue and release Morgan.

This was a man who had led his family through the most hazardous existence imaginable and yet, through it all the loving and caring spirit of his soul-mate had shone. Now she had been savagely wrenched away, leaving a gaping wound that could never again be filled or healed. Despite his best endeavours, the heart-broken husband failed to locate the remains of his loved ones, for the evil baron had cleverly covered his tracks. It might be that the enormity of the heinous crime committed in his name on that fateful day had dawned on him, and possibly out of an instinct for self preservation, he removed all evidence that could incite the hostile spirits of the Welsh people.

The loss of Gwenllian, whilst settling Maurice de Londres's local concerns to a certain extent, certainly damaged the Norman cause across the breadth of Wales. Her bravery had caught the imagination and the manner of her death made her a martyr. What is more, the previously sleeping dragon of Gwynedd was rudely awoken from its ever deepening slumber,

and this at a time when the Norman succession was ˌ
low ebb. For confusion and anarchy had become the scˑ
the Normans following Stephen's accession to the throne,
further fed the flames of the Welsh uprising. From the ˌɴorth
came thousands of warriors led by Owain ap Gruffudd (who
was to be known as Owain Gwynedd) with his brother
Cadwaladr at his side. They marched south through
Meirionnydd, confiscating or destroying anything and
everything bearing foreign imprint. As they surged into
Ceredigion, crossing over Afon Dyfi, they were joined by their
vengeful brother-in-law and nephew with a huge force of men
to swell their ranks. After careful consideration, it was agreed
that the first target to feel the dragon's breath would be
Aberystwyth Castle, the scene of the bitter struggle and disaster
that had previously halted the promising rising headed by
Gruffudd. He particularly wished to vent his spleen on the
garrison responsible for taking the life of his younger brother.

By shear weight of numbers and unmitigated ferocity, they
took the castle, slaughtered the defenders, plundered its riches
and arms, and then burnt it to the ground. As the flames lit the
early evening sky, not a blade of grass could be seen for the mass
of warriors assembled to gloat over their first major kill in the
campaign. Then, what started as a low hum rose in volume to
become an audible chant, reverberating with such power that it
could be heard by all in the surrounding district. 'Gwenllian!'
they roared, 'Gwenllian!'. This was now a force to be reckoned
with, inspired as they were by two causes; their country and
their recently martyred princess. Well had they learned the
lessons of victory and defeat in their struggle with the Norman
overlords during the past few decades. For now they fielded
heavily armed chainmail-clad knights on horse back who
formed the first effective heavy cavalry seen in Wales. Even the
infantry wore mail, a practice normally reviled by Welsh
warriors, who would in previous encounters prefer to stay light-
of-foot, more suitable for the guerilla tactics typical of Welsh

soldiery. Rather than be cluttered down by the substantial booty plundered from Aberystwyth, Owain and his forces returned to Gwynedd to shower gifts on their loved ones and brag of their bravery. Gruffudd ap Rhys became impatient, for he wanted to continue to march south and strike while the iron was hot. Soon Owain returned with vigour to purge Ceredigion and the castles of Dineirth and Caerwedros fell.

The combined Welsh forces posed a serious threat to the mightiest of Norman Lords in Ceredigion, Richard Fitz Gilbert. This arrogant man, awash in his own self importance and infallible belief in his own invulnerability, decided to travel through what was effectively occupied territory with a nervously twitching minstrel playing ahead of his small escort. He had been visiting Abergavenny and was on route to Usk Castle when a host of 'fine Gwent bowmen', led by Morgan ap Owain, unleashed a shower of deadly missiles upon them. Richard, along with all his retinue, were laid to rest on that dusty trail. When news of their fallen colleague reached his fellow Norman knights, they decided to meet force with force and assembled a huge army, ironically led by the sons of Stephen, custodian of Cardigan Castle. These were none-other than Gruffudd ap Rhys's half Welsh nephews for they were the sons of his sister Nest who, after the death of her first husband, had entered into a second marriage with another Norman lord. This however, held no concern for a man, whose sole purpose left in life was to take swift and terrible vengeance on the countrymen of Gwenllian's and Maelgwn's killers. And that is exactly what he did, when the two enemies numbering approximately six thousand on each side met head-on at Crug Mawr, just north of Afon Teifi near Aberteifi (Cardigan). This was the first time since the horror of Cydweli that the Welsh faced the foe in open combat. Again the roar rose to echo around the surrounding hills 'Gwenllian!', 'Gwenllian!', 'Gwenllian!'. Sounding like a thousand male voice choirs, they put the fear of God into the knights facing them, who were soon rocked back

on their heels having been on the receiving end of voll[e]
the powerful Welsh archers. This softening-up process ha[d]
desired effect for, when the Welsh heavy cavalry smashed int[o]
their defence walls, the rout was complete. As a bloody
memorial to Gwenllian, no fewer than three thousand enemy
soldiers were slaughtered that day with many more dying in the
panic to escape the rampant Welsh. As they retreated across the
only available wooden bridge over Afon Teifi, the sheer weight
of numbers made it collapse, drowning dozens of armour clad
men who sank like rocks to the bottom.

The remnants of this Norman force made a hasty retreat to
the safety of Cardigan Castle, a fortress that once again held out
against the concerted efforts of the advancing Welsh. The
surrounding township however, was plundered and burnt to
the ground, with a great loss of life among its inhabitants. By the
end of 1138, only the lordships of Ceredigion (Cardigan),
Morgannwg (Glamorgan) and Brycheiniog (Brecknock) eluded
the Welsh insurgence, changing once again the political map of
Wales.

The growing elation soon turned to despair, however,
because the two men who had been closest of all to Gwenllian
passed away in short succession. Firstly her father, Gruffudd ap
Cynan, described by the chroniclers of the day as, 'clever and
eloquent in several languages, noble, merciful towards his own
people, cruel to his enemies and ferocious in battle', expired at
the age of eighty-two attended by his wife and children, as well
as the Bishop of Bangor and the Archdeacon of Chester. His
remains and, eventually, those of his sons and wife were laid to
rest at Bangor Cathedral. Then, unexpectedly, his son-in-law
and devoted husband of Gwenllian, Gruffudd ap Rhys, died of
what many believed to be a broken heart. A short time after the
violent encounter at Crug Mawr, the forty-six year old
dispirited prince fell ill to an untreatable complaint - he had lost
the will to live. It was as if he wanted to join his wife in the spirit
world and, with the same determination that saw his rise to

.ed icon amongst his people, he achieved his
So died a hero amongst men who gained, and
from his adherence to the life of the sword.

effect of Gwenllian's action was plainly evident
ie end of the reign of her youngest son, Rhys ap
Gru.   fter the death of his father, Anarawd carried on the
fight to ҥad Deheubarth to freedom and this he did with admirable zeal. The unprecedented collaboration that existed between the Welsh monarchs of north and south, was to be welded into an unbreakable bond by the planned wedding of Anarawd and his cousin, the daughter of Owain. This held until the hot-headed and unpredictable Cadwaladr saw it fit to order the murder of his nephew over a territorial dispute. The shock and outrage of this irredeemable crime caused uproar amongst the family, turning brother against brother. Cadwaladr fled Wales amidst cries for his blood from his own people and especially the southerners who saw Anarawd as their 'hope, strength and glory'.

Gradually it seemed that Gwenllian was calling her family to her side in the hall of heroes, with only Morgan and Rhys remaining in the land of the living. Morgan was released sometime between Anarawd's death in 1143 and 1145, and succeeded his eldest brother to continue the family tradition. He captured Llansteffan Castle at the head of a revitalised Deheubarth army in 1146 with his thirteen year old brother Rhys at his side, experiencing the first of his many military encounters. Morgan continued to strengthen the resurgence of the kingdom until 1155. With his health and spirit failing, he decided to make peace with his maker in the traditional way through undertaking a pilgrimage to Rome for a papal blessing before he died. Unfortunately he expired en route, called by a mother who must have felt that he had been through enough hardships without having to endure such an awesome journey in his condition. Within a few years of taking the helm of Deheubarth, Rhys finally took vengeance upon the seat of the perpetrators of his mother's demise when he attacked and burnt Cydweli Castle leaving a trail of carnage in his wake.

Rhys ap Gruffudd, who gained the sobriquet *Yr Arglwydd Rhys* ruled until his death in 1197 at the height of his military prowess. Before he died, in a gesture to appease his mother's spirit, he commissioned the reconstruction of Castell Dinefwr, from where he conducted his dynamic military campaign. The fight for independence, so bitterly contested by his mother and father and consolidated by himself, gradually diminished whilst in the hands of Rhys' sons. But the bloodline proved to be strong and powerful for, about a century and a half after yr Arglwydd Rhys's death, was born another patriotic free spirit who could boast of a direct hereditary link to Gwenllian. His name was Owain Glyndŵr.

EPILOGUE

There ends the tale of our tragic princess, into whose short life was crammed more action and drama than could realistically be expected in three full lives. Much confusion reigns regarding what was her true story. Some sources gave very little information, but what they offered was often valuable because it fitted. Other sources might yield far more, but cross-checking often made the accounts worthless because of historically impossible claims. I sincerely hope that my sifting through myriads of sources, along with the application of a little reasoning and imagination, has brought justice at long last to a Welsh princess who truly deserves to live on in the memory of our nation.

BIBLIOGRAPHY

The Defenders, by David Fraser.
Who's Who In Welsh History, by Deborah C Fisher.
History Of Wales, by John Davies.
Land Of My Fathers, by Gwynfor Evans.
The Welsh People, by John Rhys and David Brynmor Jones.
Wales Through The Ages, Volume One, by Various Authors.
Heroines Of Welsh History, by T. J. Llewelyn Prichard.
History Of Little England Beyond Wales, by E. Laws.
Brut y Tywysogion, (The Chronicle of the Princes), Edited by
    Thomas Jones.
*A History Of Wales From The Earliest Times To The Edwardian
    Conquest*, by D. E. Lloyd (Volume 2).
The Life Of Gruffudd ap Cynan, Translation by D. Simon
    Evans/Llanerch - 1990.
Wales in the Middle Ages, by Catrin Stevens.
The Age Of Conquest, Wales 1063 - 1415, by R. R. Davies.
Medieval Monarchs, Editor - Elizabeth Hallem.
*Everyday Life In Wales, Book Two, From Roman Villa To
Norman Castle*, by Irene Myrddin Davies.
Mediaeval Wales, by H. T. Evans.
The Castles Of Wales, by Alan Reid.
The Battles of Wales, by Dilys Gater.

Aberffraw - birthplace of Gwenllian and historic seat of the rulers of Gwynedd. It is believed that the location of her first home (the king's palace) lies buried beneath the foundations of a housing estate.

Caeo - high in the hills of Cantref Mawr, where the remains of the thick deciduous forest still remain.

Caeo - This basin formed into the side of the hill in medieval times would have been hidden beneath the canopy of the dense forest and, arguably, could have been a possible location for Gwenllian and Gruffudd's hideout.

Cydweli Castle - The inner keep of this soon to be infamous fortress, though originally of timber construction, was where Gwenllian resided whilst carrying her first child.

Cardigan Castle - The sad remains of what was regarded by the Welsh forces as the 'toughest nut to crack'.

Aberystwyth Castle - At nearby Plas Crug, a combined Norman force from Aberystwyth and Ystrad Meurig castles routed Gruffudd ap Rhys and his followers.

Castell Dinefwr - The traditional historic seat of the rulers of Deheubarth, where Gwenllian and her forces slipped quietly by en-route to Cydweli.

Mynydd y Garreg - Seen here from a distance, where Gwenllian made her secret encampment with her followers.

Cydweli Castle - This is the distant view Gwenllian would have had of her intended target while camped at the foot of Mynydd y Garreg.

Gwenllian Monument - Has stood for nearly one-hundred years to commemorate her sacrifice.

Maes Gwenllian - this is the actual location where the epic struggle took place. Hidden in the deep grass are a circle of stones said to be where Gwenllian fell.

Battlefield - This is the perspective the Norman knights had from the upper slopes of Mynydd y Garreg. Also, to the left of the field can be seen 'Gwenllian Farm'.

Cydweli Castle Entrance - This is the location of the original draw-bridge and main entrance to the castle. It is here facing the castle ramparts you will find Gwenllian's monument, standing in open defiance to Norman rule.

Memorial Stone of yr Aglwydd Rhys - Standing at the foot of the ruins of Cardigan Castle, you will see this commemoration to the youngest son of Gwenllian and Gruffudd ap Rhys.

The Coat of Arms of Gruffudd ap Cynan - Described as: *Gules, Three Lioncels Passant in Pale Barry Argent, Armed Azure*. Seen here proudly displayed above the 'Precentor's Stall', in Bangor Cathedral. Gwenllian grew up under the protection of this powerful symbol.

Chester Castle - Within these walls Gwenllian's father, Gruffudd was placed 'out of harm's way'.

The Coat of Arms of Owain Gwynedd - Described as: *Vert, Three Eagles Displayed in Fess Or*. Under this standard Owain and Cadwaladr invaded south Wales. To its left is their father's standard and to the right is the standard of Llewelyn ap Iorwerth (Llywelyn Fawr), grandson of Owain.

Bangor Cathedral – Somewhere beneath the seating to the right of the alter, lies the remains of Gruffudd ap Cynan along with his wife and sons Owain (Gwynedd) and Cadwaladr.